Listen Up

✦

pleasant homilies
metaphorical insights
jejeune pronoucemens
plus-quotes from works never written

by

Charles E. Miller

iUniverse, Inc.
New York   Bloomington

Listen Up

iUniverse books may be ordered through booksellers or by contacting:

iUniverse
1663 Liberty Drive
Bloomington, IN 47403
www.iuniverse.com
1-800-Authors (1-800-288-4677)

ISBN: 978-1-4401-0595-1 (pbk)

Printed in the United States of America

iUniverse rev. date: 1/23/2009

Preface

Little needs to be said by way of a Preface to this volume. Most of the ideas are put as succinctly as I can write them. Some of my remarks are quite sage, others rather ordinary. Yet, in sum, they may shed a few rays of light on life as lived in America. All of the stuff herein is homegrown, right out of the earth around my house, the trees felled and the logs split by my own hands. I put a premium on originality, with pride, and so avoid any statement that smacks of borrowing, oblique reference or direct quotation, except in a few rare but noted instances outside the context of the fantastic "works." You may smile—or shudder—or throw the book away. There is a worse fate and that is being told what to think. Enjoy the book. That's why I wrote it as a compamion volume to "Now Hear This!" Cordially, I leave you and travel on.

-1-

The tines of a hayfork will ring only when they are empty. So are they like the praises of a fool.

Promiscuity is widely accepted today because it entails promises that need not be met and pleasure that need not be accounted for.

I never met a person who didn't know what he meant. What his words would lead to, that was a different matter entirely.

The shadow on the wall betrays the substance of its image. Therefore, be careful of what shape your life will take.

The dog chased the light cast by the lantern. So will you leap and spin who find ignorance a happy indulgence to be chased.

The current of the river can be accommodated only by the sweep of the boatman's oar.

If you insist upon defying death by hanging from the rock, know that the rock will never sorrow for your fall.

Hammer a nail or bend to warp. In all things give accountability.

Swept up on the majesty of the music, the fly, ancestor to man, alighted _on_ the Maestro's page to begin its serious study of the _forte._

Flaunt the ageless credo of forgiveness and you will age before your time. Anger diminishes life.

The restless honey bee seeks what it needs. How small is instinct.

"I looked and I looked and I looked—but I couldn't find any gold behind the walls."

"Then you looked—you found! Confess it!"

—from THE STINGY THIEF, by Jon McDougall, a mystery first performed at Whiteschmidt's Pentagon Theatre, Washington, D.C.

In leaching oil from the skin, salt toughens. So ought a man's condemnations of corruption toughen the social fabric by leaching out the unctuous oil of moral compromise.

Why shouldn't your life be a tidepool of living curias for your curious neighbor? After all, his secrets are too precious to bare.

A teacher of mine once told me I grinned like a Cheshire cat. In my prodigy wisdom I fancied her paranoia had momentarily possessed and overcome her.

Turn the corner and confront the issue, for a straight road is an incessant boredom.

It is said that a man's dog will howl with grief when its master dies. It understands not the convenience of death but of appetite.

If the smoke does not rise from the cabin chimney, then the air is oppressive and a storm brews. Laughter is much the same.

A sip of cold water is more precious than gold to the dying man. Why then, this shows how false to nature is material wealth.

I once lit a candle to find the door latch. Why did I not learn in the light where it was?

The miser who keeps his mouth shut reveals his heart with his purse.

A trickling cool spring on a hot mountain trail is like a kind word to the despairing. It refreshes and restores.

The higher into the branches of the tall tree one climbs, the more effort is expended to gain a vision. So it is in life—that vision must be worked for.

Beware of the dog that growls with its hackles raised. It has marked you for game.

To go abroad used to be the ambition of every young person of means. Now it is the refuge of the irresponsible or of the evangels.

"I worked my fingers to the bone for you," said the shill as she pocketed her husband's alimony. Why, there is but a small difference between the two sorts of chance—a bad marriage and a poker game.

The rise of the river forebodes acts of courage. The fall of the water augers generous deeds.

You trifle with a woman's emotions and you trifle with hell's fires and almost certain damnation.

"Keep the Home Fires Burning" was a song meant moretor the wayward husband than for the parent devoted to his progeny.

The cat vanished under the house to set up its own bivouac of love in the dark.

The constant struggle of the teacher to restore order in the classroom demolishes the love for learning.

Do not envy the wealthy. Let their pride be their richest gain and not your submissive eyes.

Keep a horse stabled and unexercised and you will soon have a sick animal. Is man any different with his sedentary lifestyle?

Be not like the snail that carries its house on its back, and knows not when it will be crushed. Let another rent thee an abode.

Eternity is for the very old and the very young. To them time lacks meaning.

A dream, a hope stalled by some insignificant quandry will perish before fruition.

No man is so benevolent that he ought to refuse a gift from another. After all, the fruited land accepts the crashing surf and gains beauty thereby.

If you get lost wait for the sun to rise for who knows but what the night brings calamity.

Satisfaction guaranteed is awfully presumptuous. I mean, can the corporation invade my flesh to warrantee such a result?

It is better to light a blaze with an honest stick of wood than to ignite the forest with a false promise.

Let the fur of the distant black bear go for the pelt of the nearby fox and you gain your fetish.

Though you shrink your neighbor's pride to its smallest dimention, appearing great and courageous in so doing, you practice the ancient cult of skull reduction. By this black magic you achieve victory.

The great horned owl stares not to be wise in men's judgment but to keep fixed upon the quarry.

Silence a barking dog and you risk robbery. Silence the mewing of a cat and you welcome mice. Silence the song of a bird and you betray ill humor.

The bellwether of political disaster is found in the presence of tolerated corruption.

Trust a man only so far as he is willing to trust you. From there on your affairs rest on faith.

I knew an old misanthrope once who dug his potatoes with a stick because he hated other men's meddling to help. And quite naturally he starved to death.

Keep to the times of harvest if you would cut the best grain.

Do not feel that you must always measure up to the standards of someone else. After all, she—or he—may be either standing on a rock or sinking in a bog.

Shortcuts are a high-level risk, whether in finance or in mountain climbing. You can lose your life at either one.

If you are hanging by your fingertips on the ledge of rock do not ask for the identity of your rescuer.

I once knew a man who learned the language through pictures. Since he thought in abstractions rather than in graphics, he turned out to be a mute.

Constant effort will often save a poor idea, just as turning the spit constantly over the coals will sometimes salvage a tough cut.

If you would destroy a nation, garble its language, water its money and obscure its history. Despotism thrives on such changes.

Do not rebuke a man for shallow reasons. He may have more to contribute to your understanding than all your sages of unmerited acclaim.

They say a person of gentle manner is often put upon by a callow world, yet his very nature is often the proof of his understanding, he having permitted the world to disadvantage itself to his amusement.

A farmer who pulled the tarpaulins over his shocks of grain sustained no loss in the winds and rain. Why ought he not to profit from his foresight?

If you wish to observe competition at its keenest yet benign to watch, throw crumbs upon the ground for the birds. This is how men compete in our world—by intimidation, power and speed.

A good bargain cannot be kept awash in a slurry of distrust for it becomes blurred, indistinct and suspect. The parties ought to begin afresh.

Maybe the cry in the wilderness is not the moaning of the wind but the pleading of a desperate man. Do not ignore it.

Science to the young, enquiring kind is as exciting as the unopened door to hinted-at treasures. Do not keep it locked for selfish reasons, as for religiousity.

"Get in, get in, get in!" (Moses cries out from the door of his ark.)

"I can's swim. The water is up to my chin."

"Hang on, hang on." (Moses revs up.) "I'll motor a round and pick you up."

—from an anarhronistic piece entitled WISPY, by Ned Noah.

"Subtract five from eight and give me two," said one lawyer to another. "I will give you one extra and charge you for the overage."

It is not the quality of the licorice that changes but the accounting of the penny.

Opportunity is sometimes like a sled on an icy hill. If you are not aboard at the top, you could miss the glide of your life.

The steam train rumbled into the tunnel unaware of its sudden demise. Is the engine of war any less for anation when its enters its timely fate?

Neighbors who square dance together stay together.

A patch of untended ill will will seed an acre of hatred.

Darkness in a cave is no less invasive than is yet another light to the sun. Sharing similitudes, they are kindred powers.

Let him who doubts the absolute principle of gravity doubt the absolute principle of Providence. You may fly but only briefly without either one.

I roared through the rapids in my frail boat. How much like trouble that roars around one, threatening the frailty of means.

Hang onto the handle of your axe in cutting life's firewood of gain or in your zeal to get warm you can injure a friend.

Conscience is like a fresh plank of wood that rarely gives up severe stains and never memories—except to death.

The fear of death is often more a matter of elevation than of survival capability.

Do not raise impossible conundrums of doubt by questioning what is goodness. The good has the blessings of an omnipotent God.

"The wrench! Mugger! Mugger, the wrench!"

"It's bloody tied to your belt, it is, gov'nor."

"Damneme, if it isn't!"

"Wot would you do without me?"

"Suffer, I guess I would, that's wot. Just ornary plain suffer."

—philosophical dialogue from BACKALLEY BLUES, by play right Conifer Jones in a One Act first performed on the Millbrae Stage, 1984.

A loose axehead is a menace to the watcher. Since precaution preventeth disaster, soak your axehead in a bucket of water overnight.

Mend the fence, pasture the cows. Skip the fence, pasture the crows.

Death is only a brief interval of uncertainty yet we try to avoid it with all our made-up uncertainties of life.

Few of life's small troubles cannot be resolved through simple courtesy.

A brick a day keeps the neighbor away.

Sloth will cure a man of every ambition but rest.

Breathes there a man who has not at some time put his right shoe on his left foot. Then we ought to forgive others errors of performance.

The philosophy of a common knot is that it provides security and continuity. A good marriage ought to be the same.

The picture of health is sometimes a portrait of death. Take care.

Why is a marble mausoleum any more honorable for a grave marker than an inscribed board up on Boot Hill? God weighs the soul of a man, not his bank account.

Along the westward wagon trail lies many an unmarked grave.

There was a touching humility and prescience to this simple burial. Dust to dust ...

Neither competition nor wealth nor avarice nor possessions can change the warp of a man's heart, for as the tree grows so is the grain set and the wood shaped. Kindness is a wood that ought to be cherished whatever the grain.

Keep no secrets, break no hearts. Keep no promises, abolish trust. Keep no possessions, worry not about things. Life is filled with tradeoffs.

The circumstances of a man's good or bad fortune are much like a journey by stagecoach in old days. One boarded regardless of the sobriety or condition of the passengers, and he arrived at his destination in either fit or poor condition.

Chance plays a great part in the accumulation of this world's goods; the smartest entrepreneur may be the biggest loser.

He who talks out of both sides of his mouth may be heeding one too many advisors.

Abrasive speech disfigures the reach of a man's image.

You must let no man deceive you with oily words. Even the undertaker is unctuous in pursuit of the crypt.

Creaking machinery demands attention. So does a rebellious spirit.

The echo of a pebble dropped into a cavern pool is like a well-chosen word: no other sound is quite like it.

Generous measure on the scales brings back the customer.

The hiss of rain on a dying fire is like drops of discouragement on a waning ambition.

"Hang onto your umbrella."

"Why?" "It's going to rain."

"Makes sense."

—from a comedy of manners entitled ECSTASY, by Henrietta Aplomb.

The rusty links of a shop sign announced <u>Patte de Fois</u>.

How quaint we have become!

A disparaging person is like a door slamming in the wind. Neither rest nor security is possible.

It wasn't that I forgot which way was North. I simply followed the south end of the needle. Be familiar with your equipment, whether a farm tractor or trail compass.

A bucketfull of sand is better than a bucketfull of pride to extinguish a braggart.

"Would you like this little chore? It is beneath Washington's fat cats to rake leaves."

"No, sir. I think I'll simply become a Congressman instead and rake the people's incomes."

"I'm in a relationship"—begins another sad story, as if the speaker is stuck in a water pipe and needs a psychic plumber to free her.

"After all I did for her she dumped me," said the sad suitor with chagrin. "I mean, oughtn't she to've first refused my gifts?"—from YE OLDE MERRIMENT, a song, Annon.

There was a flagpole sitter in my county who sat atop his perch for almost a year, advertising used autos. What won't a man go through to dispose of his rejects!

It is a tricky thing to try to deceive a good woman. You cannot tell if she is humoring you.

Take stock of your assets if you would run a railroad, for it cannot be run on ambition and dreams alone.

I yearn for the high country. What is its enchantment if not a conviviality with nature?

A puff of vanity is like a puff of wind that will blow sand into your eyes. Take care for thy vanities.

The wayfaring stranger is a fit subject for a poem or a song, but a poor risk for a sound marriage. A good romance must refrain with realities.

Put on a new roof in the summer and you are ready for winter. Put it on in the winter and you may never finish the job. There is a right time for everything.

If you'd keep the main traveled road of your life clear of obstacles, you've always got to be ready with your mules of enterprise and labor to remove them.

Neighbors whispered that it was the fantasy of old age that he had fallen in love with the young woman. Littie did they reckon that she entertained a reciprocal love for his hidden money. Thus fantasy and gold were wed.

Do not weary of giving advice if you'd acquire a plethor s of enemies. They will destroy your house of wisdom if you let them.

On the land a barking dog is greatly to be valued. Smelling a stranger it knows whereof it barks.

If God had wanted you to be totally happy He would have endorsed sin.

Keep the rims of your wagon tight because in a drought you could lose a wheel. Manage your purse in the same way.

When the rains cause the old millstream to rise, do not try to operate your grist mill. There are times when it is better to wait than to court disaster.

Who knoweth why a bird takes flight? It is a mystery that cannot be answered by "hunger."

Without oxygen a fire dies. Without love so doth the soul of a man.

"What do you say about—destiny, Jimmy? I mean you punch up your soul with them narcotics. A whiff of that grass does me in."

"Destiny is all in the imagination. That's why I do drugs."

—from *A* LESSON TO BE LEARNED, by Hieme Jason, written from Longdorf Prison, 1943.

In order to make water run uphill you must first create a vacuum. So it is that some students, once deprived of the opportunity, will learn faster than their downhill peers.

My neighbor's dog barks at ray every sound. Ought I to shoot it and offend my neighbor or throw it a bone and gratify the beast?

Do not make out of a small matter a whirlwind in the sandbox and blow the matter out of proportion to its importance.

Hold fast to that which is good—the Scriptures say. But what if the government benefits some and corrupts others? There is a dilemma here.

Do not look for a bug in the lettuce or you will off end the chef. It is better to eat the bug, since bugs are plentiful and good chefs scarce.

"Why ought I to accept your God" asked the Athiest.

"Why, it's simple," said the Parson. "God will be there regardless of your acceptance. You may as well."

—from old papers discovered in the belfry.

Work is germinal to achievemente Work is the genesis of disaster. You must be careful to discriminate goals once you are assured of the method for reaching either.

Rein in your ambition if you would not have a runaway horse.

Do you not set your day by the clock in your hallway. Well then, turn it face to the wall and become your own master.

A man who is dressed in a full suit of armor is incapable of making love to his lady. The idealism, therefore, is not in her hanky but in his willingness to become vulnerable.

The bight end of a rope is the very end to a sailor. So it should be to us who practice wrong toward others, yet we've the nasty habit of trying square knots and going on.

Do you actually think that the rain falls on the just and unjust alike? Then consider how parched is one man's field and verdant another man's.

If you will travel backwards fast enough you will soon reach your forebearers. Then you will have to explain to them your strange behavior of retreat.

"Take the wheel, Harv. I'm ready to jump!"

—from A SUNDAY DRIVE, by Max Krapp, interviewer for the "Monogehella Star Union."

It has become as popular to defame a man in public for the drama inherent in the defamation as is is to commit arson for the joy of the blaze. Both destroy once and for all.

Generosity is a virtue turned into a vice when a man stokes his neighbor's stove yet saves back no wood for his own.

A beggar treasures small coin to the degree of intensity that a rich man disdains it. The one has a shortage, the other a surplus. No government on earth has the wisdom to adjust the disparity.

The cheapening of a people's coinage and the inflating of prices unsustained by their productivity lead eventually to bankrupcy.

A penny that is no longer worth a penny reflects a dollar that is no longer worth a dollar.

He who hangs up his fiddle and his bow before the sun has set borrows a tune from idlers and the improvident.

A nation so obsessed by adultery as this can only look forward to the moral decline and bastardy of its people, from which follow impotence, strife and the death of greatness.

The travesty of illicit sex, like the glowworm in the dark soil, is not that it denies what is dark and dangerous but that it admits what is foolish and unsafe.

Why ought nature to endure the parody on procreation without producing a generation of substandard mutants?

The first inch the wheel moves begins the runaway to disaster. Therefore block the rim not with a boulder but with a stone.

The parsimonious old miser had the gall to make change from the Sunday collection plate, yet the deacons chastened him not for being too stingy but too obvious.

Covet the secrets of the night and you destroy the revelations of the day.

The mountain does not care if the hiker falls to his death yet it contrives to obliterate his footprints. There is in this slide and wash of the rock the subtle majesty of possession.

Quail feeding on wild grain justify the presence of the mountain.

Job looked into the whirlwind and saw God yet he did not forsake Him. Is any man in these days to committed to a higher authority beyond mortality.

"Do you swear the testimony you are about to give is the whole truth and nothing but the truth, so help you, P C memory bank?"

"I do,"

"Then hit the Access key and drop into place, delete 'the truth' line two. Indent tab. Let us begin. On the night.."

"Sir—?" "What is it, witness?"

"I haven't formatted my floppy, sir."

—from THIS MODERN AGE, a novel by Carte Blanche.

"Hang onto your temper, y' lousy bum!"

—a short play entitled UP IN ARMS, by J. J. Corburundum.

Although parenting is not a technique or a methodology or kindness as such, still flesh of flesh and bone of bone are far more binding than are the blessings of an impersonal court.

As the woodpecker punches its acorn into the hole in the dead bark, so ought a man to preserve his fondest memories for old age.

When the frost is on the pumpkin the orchard of winter oranges may be ruined. There are always tradeoffs in nature.

Try to treat all men with kindness. You have nothing to lose and maybe a friend to gain.

"The boy stood on the burning deck." Most boys would have jumped overboard but this boy sought glory.

It is better to suffer a flat tire on a lonely road than a woman driver in the back seat of a limosine.

Quote of a dental patient: "I got my teeth fixed today and now I can bite back." (Chewing is another matter.)

Invite the best of society to your hilltop social and there will always be a stray or two. So it is in planning a new world.

Two dogs in a tangle make one argument; so it is in a court of law. The more vicious often wins contrary to justice.

If you can find the grain of a log rail with your axe, you are well ahead of the woodsy lover who cannot fell a tree.

I once owed a man a penny for quite some time. Was it true honesty that I remembered or a bad conscience that I repaid him?

To harbor a grudge is like permitting the presence of dryrot in the foundation of a relationship.

To "fly off the handle" bears an old-fashioned relevance to loss of temper. Like a flying axehead, untrue words can be lethal.

A five-dollar downpayment can turn into a $500,000 asset. It is not the amount of the downpayment that counts but the management of the half-million dollars.

It is ironic that a mask will sometimes deceive the wearer of it.

Since the worm knows the hole it has crawled from, send all destructive thoughts back to their source.

I can hear the distant clap of thunder but can do nothing about it. This, too, is like revolution in the streets or anarchy at the hearth.

As the boomerang returns to its thrower, so does ill will, a wrong word or perverse judgement return to its speaker.

The small things in a person's life can be either termites or diamond dust. It all depends upon one's perceptions as to causes.

Do not neglect to mend your roof between storms, whether finances, possessions or human feelings.

The narrow is not always straight. Whoever said it Was has never climbed a mountain.

As a fire burneth in the hearth so are a man's days in the retreating and the waning and the dying.

To steep your senses in self-indulgence is to imbibe the wine of self-deception.

All goodness in a person comes to nothing when they curse the day of their birth.

Find me one good man who honors his country's past and I'll show you a hero.

If you fail to hit the nail-head of the dilemma with the hammer of your reason, then you lack skill both in dialogue and in argument.

The people standing along the way tossed flowers on the catafalque. Little did they know the man therein was their dreaded enemy. How often people worship the ceremony without the significance.)

The Egyptian Sphynx has gained fame by her silent riddle. It ought to be the same with a man's past.

If you take the trouble to walk down to the creek, why do you take the trouble to return? That is a conundrum.

As the snow clothes the scene oft giving beauty to ugliness, so ought a man's kindnesses to redress the wounds of another.

"And where is he?"

"He's left me." "And why did he leave you?"

"I dumped him." "Then wipe your own tears."

—from a pity party letter, annonymous. This is a common scenario for stupidity or naivete. Any common alley cat would react the same way as the loser.

How men scoff at those quirks of mind that *seem* to them weak, irresolute, ill defined and vacillating! Do they make chance the god who orders exactly 52? Who declares the rules, the equipment, the fun of the game?

It was said of him that he lost his marbles in the game of life. Could it be that he ignored the ring for the other players?

Better a set of false teeth at the banquet than the finest dentines and an empty stomach.

It is a wiley fox that smells the man-snare amid the grapes. Why trouble the animal with your imprecations?

Let the rains come. My fields are planted, ditches dug, cistern ready and cattle thirsting. Thus speaketh the man who prepares in life.

Any bird that creates its own filing system is uncommonly smart.

A budget without a deficit is not a beast of burden to be loaded up with the whimsical investments of squanderlust.

A struck timber may produce the powder of its decay. In this way strike your government with criticism as a citizen.

Safety is not the sole measure of one's security, but, instead, precautions.

The bureaucrat seems to be a necessary corruption for the Federalist state and yet how many of his servicing borers are required to destroy the hull wood of the vessel?

I love the grain of many kinds of woods whether quarter sawn or cross-bucked. I like to view people by these standards. In some the rings of security show, in others the striations of struggle.

Shrinking wood will open cracks in the wall, much a s shrinking courage will admit disparagement and defeat.

There is an anger that is selfish and a wrath that is righteous, and now even good men can always tell the difference.

Honor is not like a wheel of fortune that, once broken, comes around again. It is given to each person only once in life, yet more often than not does he wantonly throw it away., That is tragic.

"On the way to the market I lost a penny in the street drain—and that's my contribution to the wealth of the community," said the miser.

The beggar'. dirty, quivering hand, out-stretched, asks not for thy soul nor thy purse nor thy possessions—but only for a coin.

Although bad company can corrupt good speech and maaners, good speech can sometimes correct bad company.

Hear the cheerful sounds from thy neighbors yard and repent of thine own misanthropic temper.

A road without ruts is little used. So develop the ruts of experience in a man's life that mark his way.

The person who is slack in his work is often given t o dreams without accomplishment. He imagines that the barn is already built and the fields harvested.

Do not trouble your neighbor with your own or he will, soon enough, build a wall against your invasions of his contentment.

The power of reason is like unto the strength of wood. Some kinds are stronger, more dense, easier to work and resistant to termites and decay. Think about it.

He whose aim can strike a match at 100 yards ought to guard the king. Or the president.

Listen carefully into the shaft of the mine in a man's life. Is it more than wind that moans deep down therein?

"Far be it from me—" is an old adage expression for a man who cozens his neighbor and covets his small cash possessions.

The ways of the wicked are straight and good in their own eyes. It is a waste of time and breath to oppose theme

Dishonest conduct is better than dishonest speech for it is harder to hide the former.

Do not divulge all thy private affairs to a friend, for no man is so honest that he will not be tempted to steal from thee.

Eschew the pietists who say all is for hought without fishing for men's souls. Civilizations great advances were not created by churchmen. Besides, God did not command you to specialize.

Illumine your life with the Word of God, unless you find merit in stumbling in the dark. One needs only a candle of interest in its truths.

Keep well, for thou canst not chop wood with a lame back.

A good idea dropped thoughtlessly amid indifferent company is like a silver coin cast into a deep well. I t can be seen, perhaps, but does no good to anyone.

"Snake eyes!"

"Box cars I"

"Little Joe from Kokorao!"

"What're you guys doing?."

"We're working our way through life, sir.,"—from THE CORRESPONDENT, by Salvage de Marks, ret. for "The Eagle."

Only God knows the wing of what bird in flight dropped the blue feather. Is one's mistake or excess that important that others ought to know—whose blue feather?

The craftsman who saws to the line is like a leader who wastes no materials. Each is a craftsman in his own way. Both are creators from raw stuffs.

The lineliness of a farmer and his wife often produced a nights lodging for the wayfarer—and the news. The exchange was apt and trusting.

Manliness has nothing to do with copulation, braggadocio, gunfire or knife fights. It has everything to d o with moral courage from which arise true strength and moral stamina.

Leadership, true leadership, is not jerking and leaping and playing the lead dog in the traces of the sled, but is the capacity to utilize the talents of subordinates for a coordinated effort.

For the want of a nail a timber fell. For the want of a timber the house collapsed. For the want of a house the man was homeless.

A man who cheats a friend at cards bears a hidden grudge.

Be wary of such as he.

It was a silly tale of extravagance that the rich man invested in flower gardens. Yet the world wore a path t o his door to look upon the beauty he had grown.

The loss of a loved one is like the loss of an old homestead: the tangibles go but the memories never perish.

Time is nothing to youth, it is everything to age. Now I no longer wonder why old achievers play.

"Burn the library down!" cried the vandals, and all the judges clapped in unison and murmured, "We honor their freedom of expression in doing so."

Wood will dry and shrink in the incessant burning s u n. How much like a man's brain is submission to sterile ideas!

The messenger of bad news is less to be dreaded than is the bringer of tidings of joy. For the one can tell n o worse but the other informs about what is transient.

Keep thy boots clean and thy boots will keep thee.

If trees were made of precious metal, a pound of wood would be worth more than a pound of silver. Scarcity is everything.

Do not wrap up the test too soon or you may leave out the final ineluctable answer.

-2-

She engaged the seer to fortell her life and so threw away natural instincts for a glass bauble.

A man and a woman were created for their oneness. Two of a kind are forever separate.

A roan'8 capacity for sacrifice rarely equals a woman's.

Does the coyote know that the housecat is a friend o f the housedog. distant canine relative?

Only a circus clown will try to ride a horse backwards. This much can be said of a person who is filled with regrets.

Careful navigation steers the course of ambition.

When the evolutionist rejects purpose in the universe he gives his argument a mortal blow. Instinct is blind.

Some say we have evolved from fish—but how did they thrive without wishing to become man?

Like a surgeon carving out a tumor from the flesh, you must cut beyond the visible line in a relationship in order to remove the moribund part.

Courtesy is never out of fashion in a man's treatment of a woman.

Be careful of the man who will spend freely yet is unable to pocket his pride. There is in him a serious contention in values.

A guest well chosen for the night is like a select bottle of wine. Both speed the time along on wings of contentment .

There is something about a long beard that troubless. Does it inspire fatherhood or thought or criminality?

The mysterious professional economist is at best a guesser, at worst a prophet. Believe neither. Spend when it is safe to do so and save when it is not.

"Where do you go?" asked the steam engine of the donkey.

"To my master's house to be fed. And thee?" asked the donkey.

"Why, to obey without intelligence what my master commands ."

"How sorry I am for you," said the donkey. "You d o not even have the option of escape." Thus is slavery without mind.

A log without a fire in the hearth is like a man without a good wife to love.

A woman who wants what she wants is hard to beat. It is even more difficult to amend her nature.

After a hard ride, a hard drink. After a hard drink, a hard bed. After a hard bed, hard times.

Statesmanship requires that one promite the welfare o f the country and of the people before his own.

The lust for power is sure to guarantee a hedgeraony among equals.

Like cleaning your chimney flue to prevent an attic f ire purge your conscience of dross to avoid the combustion of guilt.

I feel an affinity with a barking dog. We both know and sense the alien footstep. I may forgive the trespass but it cannot. There is a certain wisdom in animals.

To reach a compromise without an initial consensus is to start a fire with wet wood and a dry match or a w et match and dry wood. It makes little difference who is right to begin with.

Do not berate the beggar for his lack of an abode a t night, for what have you to do with him lest he be indebted to you?

You cannot censure hatred with a willow switch. You must subvert the motives from below ground.

Like an old injury mindlessly kept turning over the blaze, repentance ad nauseum prevents healing forever.

He who shoots a deer with a crooked arrow trifles with sacred life. God-created its value derives from His hand.

A loud voice that echoes in the mountains is worse than a chafing wound to the spirit of quiet.

He who bangs at the outer gate demanding entry at on c e is suspect in his motive. Is it anything less when a government intimidates its citizens by absurd laws?

Mend the old board fences to thy accounts lest you lose what little stock remains.

In bequeathals make allowance for adversity.

"Which is it to be. my dear—a bird in a guilded cage or a hawk on a craggy ledge?"

"Are you offering me—things or love?" "Neither, my pet. I am offering you freedom or captivity. Each has its price."

—from THE SHOWOFF, a play about taboos and mistreatment.

I once took a young lady paddling in my canoe. Little did she realize I was heading for the open sea. Sometimes we go too far.

"Catch the end of that rope!" I shouted down at him. "But do you know who I am—a wizard, a champion!" "Then my rope is not good enough for you. I will take my rescue efforts somewhere else."

—from WINGS IN THE WIND, by Jerome Statz, "The Trumpet."

My cousin said to me, "Take good care of aunte. She is all you have of your father.. clan, and you know where they have all gone."

"Any man who fails to scrape the mud from his boots shall not enter my house. Dirt and X are enemies," said t he spinster and this maketh man my foe.

Never counsel indifference toward human suffering.

Regardless of the integrity of the jury tolerance of a crime is like a court without a judge for justice is at risk.

The true test of quality is not one man's standards but a harmony of performance.

The way of the rat is secretive. Why ought 500 millions of Chinese and Hindus worship such a creature and dignify it with diety and holiness?

It may be possible to dance with seven in a square but it is the eighth dancer who gives significance to the call.

Custom begs its following by practice.

Chicken delights the tramp, quail titillates the hunter's palate, squab impassions the connoisseur and duck entices the experienced eater. What they all have i n common is not their taste but their appetites. Who shall arbitrate?

In building a log house, chop the mortice in the saddle corner with precision and a sharp axe or the shrinka g e will weaken the wall. Too bad that we cannot measure a ad cut the events in our lives with the same precision— or is it?.

All things need not be confessed to one's wife. Aft e r all, you do not burn the furniture of inheritance to keep the house warm.

Any man who cheated on his wife was once deemed a disgrace. A woman who cheats is nowadays thought needful . Between the need and the disgrace lies a no-man's land which none cross without harm.

Notice the flight patterns of different birds. Some will skip about others fly from point to limb, still other s wheel and circle as if to reconnoiter. This is remarkable to one who walks in the woods.

Bickering over money is like the quarrel of two dogs over a bone. Usually the stronger one wins, unless the weaker is faster.

When the knot falls out of the board the floor become s perilous. So is a faulty plank in politics.

The rapping of the woodpecker that breaks the silence of the forest makes no apology for being himself.

"I can't stand my chauffeur. I simply can's stand him."

"Then fire him."

"Oh. but I couldn't do that. You see—he's related t o the Marquis de Neully."

"A nobleman out of pocket, I presume." "No, a beggar out of noble blood."

"Then I suggest you raise his pay, madame."—from THE SNOBBERY OF CIRCUMSTANCES, by Amadon Gant,II.

A woman once told me she kept few secrets from her husband, but I think he was much upset and bent out of shape by his wife's honesty.

I saw him crouch on the rock, ready to dive into the swirling foam of the rapid and I thought, "How magnificent his pose! How generous his readiness! How noble his ambition." But then the cries for help soon ceased and the rescuer retired.

"Put the pot of broth over there and stir up the fire some. Your father will be home before dark, and he'll be wet and tired from his journey—and hungry, to boot."

"He does not lack an appetite for travel, I see." "Hush, child, it is not for you to condemn your father for wanting to collect on old debts."

—from A WAYFARING PA, by Jules Schmidt (3 acts) Pogrom Publishers.

A man's true character will emerge from hard circumstances like a photograph in the developer. First, the shadows a ad then the highlights, the dark concealments and then the brighter revelations.

Experience is often an apt teacher until the student makes that experience a substitute for his or her new discovery.

-3-

As the ferrier smooths the horn of the horse's hoof with his rasp, so ought a man to smooth the horn of his enemy's displeasure with firm words.

But first you must listen for the ring of the anvil to discover the shaping vision.

Play with a gun and toy with death. Play with God and toy with life.

A thorn in the paw of a dog will cause it to limp. S o is hate a festering sort to the true walk of a man.

Service to others is less a matter of your choice than it is of their necessity. That comparison ought to fraraeyour attitude.

If you stay on the trail long enough you're sure to meet somebody of like mind.

Sex came along with the young generation. Before that, folks good folks at least, were just hatched.

If your staked claim infringes on another's diggings, you can be sure you'll hear from him. The concept of "personal territory" is not altogether new.

Pool's gold is visible and floats on top of the slurry; the heavier real gold must be dredged up. So are some me n. s minds like one or the other.

It is not the ambition that corrupts; worthy men have achieved great things through ambition. But it is the scurvy devices of subterfuge and cheating that erode honor in the striving.

Keep a secret, defend a friendship.

The laundry hanging on the clothes line flapped in the wind waiting for its new assertions.

When the rain came and filled the bucket by its drip from my roof, I thought— too late—of repairs. So does hardship come upon a man while he idles.

Love money, hate love.

At eleven thousand feet I left the forest behind and entered the rare domain of the gods, where the air is pure, the silence soothing, the solitude enfulfing. He who walks alone in the heights knows of what I speak.

Fish in troubled waters and you may catch a shark. W hat then?

If you have a faith hold fast to it. At least it is a sheet anchor in stormy seas.

Do not let wicked men scorn yout youth to show their power over you. Reject their opportunism out of hand, for they have neither earned wisdom nor merited dominion.

There is no ploy that more disaffects a man from the society of the saints than do lies. Yet they are a basket of snakes in the formal church nowadays.

Keep your fantasies alive. Let not ignorant men quench your dreams. Cultivate the vision that is indifferent to jealousy and destruction. This is your birthright.

The eevil hangs on every word of the sophist. He knows the true value of deceit.

On a windy hill I flew a kite into the air, yet it crashed plummeting into the treetops from too much string. To o much greed, too little lift.

The Senator was afflicted with squanderlust; he scorned the labor that earned the dollar.

The mad stationmaster waved his hand in the wind as t h e. train roared by, thinking he had something to do with its power. .

"Run, run!" cried the schoolmaster to the boy, "If there's a rabbit on your heels it will catch you for sure." I n this way wisdom teaches innocence how to escape living.

"Why should I keep an old man waiting, rocking away in a chair on his porch?" death asked. "Simple," quoth he." Duration is more a product of will than of time. I'm whit tling my epitaph."

The great horned owl sits on the ledge above my head, wisely scanning my lines. Ought I to invite him into my consolations?

I walk through the frosted grass of each new day, never to return the same way.

Hospitality was once a byword along America's rural roads. Now it refers mainly to money's insurance.

The beggar was free of debt but panhandled for a meal. The roch man was loaded with debts but nibbled on dainties. There's a paradox there.

I fell to my death once but God caught me in the foliage of a tree. I stepped *over* the precipice of a rock fall but God dumped me into the scree slide,, I miscalculated the tenacity of a rock once, but God gave me a shrub t o grab. What can you say about such escapes?

Never do the angels entertain greed but only necessity. How else can one account for their appointment by God?

Five cents worth of accomplishment is worth carries far more weight than a dollar's worth of braggadocio.

Constancy is not so much a thing of the past as it is an ideal scarcely attained these days. By quenching its novelty, its value is maligned.

Do not make merry when the widow mourns for her drunkard husband. Was she not a part of his sad end? Therefore, observe and solemnly agree with her—the bottle and not her ambition marinated him.

"Fifteen feet of rope will tether that animal," said the rancher of his feral dog. What confidence in the unpredictable!

When hammering on a nail watch not the shadow of the crow lest you mar the wood.

Trust a judge with your life and regret the surrender o f your conscience.

A man with the mouth of the lion will bleed for the lives of his whelps.

No man who is ever fully contented with this world will amount to a pile of rocks—which at least provide a sanctuary for snakes.

"I have lived long enough in this world, my dear Peter, to see in every ambition the seed of distruct, in every victory of the vote the pangs of temptation, and in every willful neglect of high office the disrespect for the charge, howsoever latent, of incipient perjury."—Marlene as the so-called Witch of the Corridors in COME TO MY HOUSE, by Christine Webb.

Spit into the fire of a man's wrath and its hiss only mails the heat thereof, not the diminution of the flames.

"Do you condemn that man who was so lately hung by h is own testimony to hang twice? Now, sir, the double jeopardy rests. Let his conscience plead its own case." an anecdote in THE PIRATEER, by Quagsmith, a Scrivener.

The fragrance of a woman's inner beauty will follow her long after the petals have fallen.

Do not try to unmake the worst of life's ills and mistakes but instead, like the eagle building her nest, seize what remaining twigs and straw can be used to best advantage.

"Go and sin no more," admonished the Priest, "but if thou sinnest remember—open the door to repentance and give sup to grace."

—an old church record, discovered in remodeling St. Albans.

The man who is unhappy with his lot in life will easily find a place to put in his shove^ Let him dig to find his peace.

He who contemplates suicide finds mirth in death; he who contemplates living finds death in life. In these circumstances the catalyst is faith, not action,, Triumph i s slow. Be calm and endure.

Keep to the rutted way, dear Charmu, and you will feel the road beneath the snows of winter.

Barefoot and pregnant isn't so bad when you consider the opposite—well-heeled and sterile.

The ravenous wild animal seeks only what will. satisfy it s hunger. Rapacity is the invention of man.

Plant a compliment in the ear of a maiden and grow a child.

"NO FENCE JUMPERS" read the sign beside an especially luxuriant pasture . Problem was you could read it only from the inside.

Let no man mock your learning when he has little or non e of his own to offer.

A mind once closed and locked by bigotry is ranely, if ever, pried o pen by a visible justice of right.

The coyote is more clever than coward, more elusive than deceitful, more enduring than submissive. He is maligned because he echoes the depravity in man's nature.

Do not shingle your roof in the rain, my son, lest people think that you are either mad or improvident.

Forgiveness rarely begs thanks from an ungrateful man. B y doing so it perishes in its pride.

'Ever hearitell how the Buckhorn Pub got rida them what wuz too rowdy? Barkeep'ud put 'em out to root round wit their country cousins, yessiree."

—John Pareifal.s new book BESIDES, Cord-n-Knot, Pubishers.

Obsessed by the boundaries of his ownership and and trespassers upon the land of his contentment, the old farmer was always mending his fences when the posts and rails were sound.

Like mules, some folks have a suspect geneology though their strength is great. A mule is a more useful animal than a thoroughbred in the farm country.

Like a climb up a greased pole, there's nothing to compare with trying against impossible circumstances.

A sharp tongue like a sharp drawknife can peel an argument thin.

The missing stone in the wall was honored by the play o f a child at war.

As the lichens grow in the dampness of the rocks, s o do old premonitions emerge and prove harmless, occult and silent over the granite surface of the years.

"Let no ambition steal your character, sir—or cripple the honesty your constituents know you by. If you aspire to office, take her for all the love for integrity you possess."

—Paul Cunningham in "The Cache of Dishonors," a story.

Do not let life's gyppos blow the horn of doubt into your ear or, with the increase of your deafened discernment, you will turn to their sleaze for direction.

"Halt!" Jerome cried aloud as he cocked his magnum revolver and fired one round into the bark of the nearest tree. The mere flash produced the desired result."

—from "Johnny Applecore," by Wm, MeWilliams, playright.

It is the moustache and not the lip that keeps the upper lip stiff. Few persons with real courage are clean-shaven.

Cozy up to the steam calliope and let its merry shrieks and whistling steam blasts rivive the saner past.

One world? Come now. Mister President, you are not the Messiah to accomplish this, although the gold that you cherish may buy the illusion. The drift is cultic. Utopian.

Common policies have done more than diplomacy to chain the desires of our allies to our fanciful dominion. And yet the links of friendship, in history past, have dissolve d in the acid of disillusionment.

Be wary of such a fellow who overworks "incredible," for he may falsify the good news by hyperbole.

The patina on old gold gives it value. Do not polish away the tarnish of common wisdom from sage advice.

"Do you mean to stand there with your face hanging out and tell me you bought a junk car for five dollars? Well, I hope you. rebettern some of these five-dollar drivers I seen around this town."

—from "Tailspin," a farcical tale about the anonymous auto driver.

The best buyer for a pig in a poke is the lazy gambler. I mean—you either got chittlings or a pregnant sow for a dollar.

Do you wish to make a million by the time you are forty? Aim not at the cache of gold but at the profundity of human needs.

Prepare for winds of dislike by honoring yourself with accomplishment.

Submit your gifts to the world's idols and face the prospect of annihilation.

"Taste not, want not," said the country wise-acre. "All depends on the dish, baby. Sight alone's cured many a appetite,,"

—from BARGAINS, a throw-away shopper's guide.

If you listen to the bum steer of a well-meaning neighbor, you may harvest your crops in the rain, when the moon is shrunk and the snows threaten.

Once you've lit the candle in the darkness, work through the night till it burns to the stub.

What is a writer's block if it is not his intention t o quit in contention with his desire to continue?

Owe no man anything, not even his lawnraower, lest he take you to court for deprivation, job loss, emotional distress and sue you for your house.

"Sun, them Yankees've come down here to make luv to our women, steal our fahms from us by crook or hook and any other legal processes—and 'ud put us to the harness if it wasn't for our President. It is not slavery that's the issue, sun, but rivalry. No two ways about that'un."

—lines from the 4-Act tragedy entitled, "The Big Crawdad Fisherman," opened Empire Mine Theatre, 1913.

Like the words of denegration and the taunts of levelers, the winds of abuse high on the mountain will tear at your tent shelter.

"You'll never learn the ropes of this ship by hanging onto the bight end of one sheet."

—from "The Mariner's Companion," edited from a diary by Hendricks Marcussen, 1st Mate on "The Cleopatra"out of Boston, 1878. She was a clipper merchantman.

"What a sweet, beautiful song dost thou bow on thy instrument, good woman. What is it—a dulcimer, a viola, a n Irish harp?"

"No, good sir, it is my husband who answers ray every touch."

—from a 17th Century play "The Breadwinner," by Altura Soporwith.

America is the only nation in the world that makes of a deadly disease a virtue to proclaim. And all the world said, "Hey, man!" Were there more shame there might b e less disease.

Be cautious regarding the simple nature of appearances. At the other end of the trail the spoiler may lie in wait for you to trip his snare. The Indian understood this.

Like the blunt edge of a wood axe that bounces off the log, so is a dull mind against a sound idea.

Do not cherish what is surrogate but treasure what is real.

"Does your cereal snap, crackle and pop when it ought to bang, crack and pumpch? Beef up your morning's bowl with POGROM, the cereal of daily liquidation. 10 rubles per pkg."

—graffiti on a Leningrad wall.

"Do your teeth gleam in the dark? Are you missing out on instant romance? Do your creditors deplore your b a d breath? Try PHOSPHORESCENCE, the toothpaste of happiness and smile with importance."

—from "The Advertiser." (free)

Few folks that I know of keep their dogs in the bedroom, but a few dogs that I know about keep their owners indebt.

In the marketplace thank those who ought to be thanked. In the quiet of your lodgings count the coin of other men's deceptions.

Go ahead and shingle your roof with torn regrets and lapsed promises and see if the rainstorm of memories doesn't flood out your inner peace and comfort.

"The hour grows late, the oil in the lamp burns low and still—still I hear in the kennels the problems of state yap and bark for solution. 'Peed them,' you say, Senator., What, by the grace of God—empty promises, sugared hopes, lofty sentiments?"

—from "Visitor at the Gates," by Whitcomb Mallory, English playwright.

Spite is its own victor which feeds on the loveless soul of its possessor. Therefore, my child, do not give way to those inner urgings of revenge and so perpetuate the malaise.

Life grows increasingly harsh in a society that lauds criminals, rewards corruption and applauds what is perverse. Common courtesy becomes obsolete, wimpish and of little value.

How some folks chew on the calamities of others, as if the pain of a neighbor who shot his horse were of greater import than the joy of the man who butchered his wife.

"It don't take no brains to hoe weeds but it sure do r e-quite some teeth to eat taters."

—little volume of "Country Wit & Wisdom" (1806)

The barking dog is only a momentary nuisance but the material loss to the robber is a permanent memory.

California's gift to the world is gold. Not even climate will inspire men to cross the rubicon of decency to live here.

"I once played the part of a dead zoo keeper," he told me.

"How was he killed?" I asked. "By the anger of an IRS ape."

"Now he truly must be dead," I replied. "No—merely translated into the 1040 form."

—from on-set dialogue with the director of "The Great Feed Disaster," a box office flop as well it deserved to be.

In the quest for facts about evolution, I find a miner's struggle with his stubborn burro more entertaining and far more instructive of reluctant human nature to change than-

—let us say—instinct.

Eastern malarky comes in three sizes: pre-Colonial. Colonial and Banker's Model. We in the West have had the most to do with the last one.

"I'll never make it," said the glow worm who then promptly went out.

"I will, I will," said his friend, who basked in t h e light of others, claiming originality and enlightenment.

If you keep that man knocking at the door any longer, h e will claim ownership of a portion of it—that which his fist touches.

Walking toward the town one night I found a silver coin lying in the dirt of the road—a shibboleth of small blessing spun off from the darkling moon.

Radical surgery on the egos will salvage some relatinships.

"Better to eat squid blindly in the fo'cstle than crow in the crows nest where all the world is the judge of your vision," said the leader of the turtles.

Sorrow is like the wound of a limping leopard. Its beauty follows after, its passion is contained, its natural quest is for seclusion and rest and healing.

In the treeless high mountain pass, where the wind chills to the bone yet few men travel thither, rejoice in the moment. It is a pure gift from prodigal nature and the provident hand of God.

He who accepts the sadism of another is caged.

More women in history would have been martyrs had men acklowledged their spiritual equality. Joan d'Arc was one o f them—as were nameless female spies in the Civil War.

"Let the accused hang for his own infamy, since it's plain he would destroy the opinion of greater men by his attacks on their honor."

—from "The Justice of the Maelstrom," by Thos. Cromwell, a plea at the Temple .

"I never played a game of horseshoes with that man but what he tried to cheat me a inch or two at the stake. The n I hired him and he cheated me out of my land."

—from "Little Things," a skit by Clairvoyance, Esq.

All of life, if lived fully, is a grueling dogsled race to the finishline, in which those who help, the frosted dogs, must be cared for, but those who lose are never mourned."

—from THE MIRROR OF SACRIFICE, a novel by Jess Norden.

"Whoa!" said the blind man driving his horse through the town.

"Gee!" cried the visionary who saw a better turn in the road.

"Haw!" entoned the therapist thinking of the poor horse. Only the lone bystander saw that the horse was sigbtless yet knew the way to the barn unaided and by the common instinct of its nature.

To this day I think our government does not understand the value of work that translates into wealth.

When British men-of-war shanghaied American seamen, they got what they asked for—a fight. Dolly Madison's dinner table set for her President Husband greeted the invade r s of Washington with mockery.

Dogs will fight over a bone not to test their skill in combat or to satisfy their hunger but to answer to instinct. Why train beastiality when it lacks intelligence?

Hold on tight to the wheel of reason and the sheet of logic if you. d tack through the choppy waters of political debate.

Do not try to halt the bronzed horse of outraged public o-pinion or you may wind up engraved.

Be wary of that person who is fattened on scandalous compliments. They can be anathema to a genuine trust of him.

"Navigation on water to me was always a matter for the fishes to supervise and man to let alone. Thus did I surrender early in life a career as a global explorer."—from the diary of John Edgeworth, 12th Century cartographer.

Hold fast to that rope which is well anchored.

Consider the little spider how it dangles in space between upspinning and down raveling. Does it not challenge danger by instinct. 0. that man should do as well!

Do not crush out an old love like a rose but instead le t the fragrance sustain thee for as long as it will.

I knew a man once who painted himself into a corner. Blythely he retreated, covering his tracks with fresh paint.

A judge of my acquaintance sawed off the limb that he s at upon. Now I know why his bad judgement collapsed of its own weight.

A good marriage is a mutual commitment. A strong marriage are the ties therein. A radiant marriage sounds its constant theme of love. And a lasting marriage is self-abnegation before God.

A husband who bribes his wife to remain faithful distrusts her. This adventure ought to be clear at the start,,

At the sacred altar they said, "I do." In the bedroom they said, "I must." In the grave they said, "I did." How empty their intentions!

Do not trifle with a young woman's emotions thinking you will use her. For in doing so you erode your integrity.

Many souls look to God to make up for their deficiencies in faith. That He should be so generous and complaisant!

Stoke a wood stove with green wood and raise the chill smoke of impatience.

From a distance, down in the valley, I saw the tendril of smoke rise into the autumn air. It feathered the head of a quiet household.

An axe struck to its helve will bind in a green logo In a like manner is a hasty and ill-considered answer in a quarrel hard to retrieve.

Poverty is like a wedge oft driven by circumstances between the oath of trust and the damnation of rebuke.

No human vision is sacred, except that of the Godhead.

We live in an age of ingratitudes. Is it not strange that they mock some of man's finest qualities—charity, trust, hope and love? These are imponderables that do not beg.

Do you really think you can cheat on the devil and win heaven's love? That is a quaint humor.

You cannot teach a rebellious child to obey a senseless reproof. He will always find the alibi for his way.

A baldheaded old buzzard I knew taught by avoidance—of ritual, cant, pain, deprivation and rank rewards—thus living to put the priest, gossip, doctor, poorman and Senator into their graves.

To a rebellious individual authority is less a factor in government than it is in human stupidity.

Courtship, the Parson said, must invite luminous doubt's as to one's own worth. This is not disesteem or self . flagellation but a pragmatic honesty.

"I don't ever want to see you again," she said.

"Why not?" he asked.

"Because your overconfidence about life frightens me. The world is not so well ordered as you suppose."

—from "Dilapidation," a play by Franz Marqu.

"If you don't believe in God, then why do you worship the Fuhrer?"

"He is <u>the</u> god," said Jorge.

"But don't you see—if you accept a god that is human, you must admit to the existence of god in your life, human or spiritual—and one is as conceivable as the other is real."

—from "The Revolving Turret," by M. Hoblein (Ger.)

"Give me your hand in marriage. "

"You're too old fashioned for me, Larry."

"Yes| but if marriage has gone out of fashion so has the commitment of love."

"Love can exist without commitment."

"Love is commitment—they're exchangeables—even of t h e crudest sort. Shoot a man's horse and you'll discover the depth of his attachment."—from "A Prisoner of Lust," by Zendel Swabel.

Why ought a wife to submit to her husband?—is one of the questions of this age. One must define the parameters o f the submission to answer the question. Know this, however, that contention for the leadership will destroy a marriage. Agreements are legal, leadership is voluntary.

The coyote sniffed at the bait and retreated from harm. The dog, salivating with hunger, threw caution aside a n d sprang the trap.

Though the toys of a grown man are his many loves, the toys of a grown woman are her many men.

Wisdom, quoth the barn owl, is not the steady gaze of my visionary eyes but the security of my taloned clutch.

Bear false witness and spring the trap of judgement.

"Instruction," said the woodpecker, "is but a little putting away for worse times."

Lie once, cheat thrice -thyself, thy neighbor, and thy God.

A man who bears false witness ignites a fire, instills a plague and confronts the bear.

Scoffers, owing little fealty to this world, solemnize the absurd. Thus the titmouse builds her nest of rags.

Scorn what is good and just, then earn what is wicked and wrong.

A boy taught once honors his teacher.

A boy taught twice honors himself.

A boy taught thrice honors his country.

Be slow to anger—unless the ship is sinking. There will be time for lullabyes.

The wisdom of detachment, said the old sourdough, will keep a man's druthers iced up for life. Preserving his candor for prompt use brings warm rewards.

Fear of God is not a weakness but a candid admission o f one's limitations. God just happens to hold the surplus.

A child's laughter is a rebuke to a man who cannot tolerate his own soul.

Galloping off into the blackness of the night, fear struck the horseman dumb, yet he did not turn back. In due course the moon of reason lighted his way.

Instruction is the yoke of the teachable,, the curse of the indifferent.

A fierce generation stirs the fuming caldron of enmity . Even friends parteth.

A prudent man is like a fishing grizzly bear that knows where the current of the river runs too swift.

Even the charaillion is given to change, yet the truth of its color is not hid.

Do not take refuge behind the invisible part of a half truth. Like a broken stone wall, the missing stone s will be found.

"You wish to conjure up hatred of thy soul to test its mettle, nay, its very existence. Then spread lies and slander and evil rumors and see how the world accepts thy oblations."—from PRIEST OF CIRCUMSTANCE, by Carrum Magnussun. A play.

In times of deep self-doubt be wary of the soothing w o rd of an avowed friend. Neither can pain be so easily assuaged nor can understanding be so hastily granted. Silence worketh a greater balm.

"Plague take it! Where are my suspenders?" railed the fireman while the house burned down.

"Tarnation!" swore the whitehaired old man. Keep your convictions turned right side out and your squabbles wrong side in.

"I'd rather shoe a horse with three legs than listen t o that Congress feller argue for solid four-legged taxes."

—Anon

Wealth—what is it? said the rich man. Wealth—where is it? asked the poor man.

"When the moon crosses the apex of the toof topssee there—old Machant's dwelling—you're to sweep down up—on the town and mercilessly kill the dogs of revolt."

—a plaintive line from "Bloody Sanction," by Port Cullis.

A man of prudence bargains with a whisper and barters with a wedge.

Given to change, flee from the real.

Witness to the truth the Chamber will rise. Witness to the false you sully the skies.

A night of poker, a day of wishes.

Know mercy, claim love; scorn love, earn hate.

"Keep your feet dry or you'll catch your death of cold, . Sara said with that gentle irony of assertion that knows life from death and—at least one—of its causes. "

—from "The Scandalous Three," a story by Jennie Kingston, writer.

Luck is no more than the application of trial and error, thus its appeal to pragmatic Americans. What used to be attributed to <u>God</u> is assigned to inoffensive amoral <u>luck</u>.

"Trade you my bony cow for your waddling sow," said the farmer to his neighbor.

"It's a deal," said he and they dido The sow littered and littered and littered; the farmer became a hog rancher. The cow dropped dead from a heart attack the next day and so did her owner—which goes to show there's a certain salutary value to barter in the marketplace.

Do not fit every key on your ring to try the lock. Know the one that works, like a writer adept with words.

The wisdom of the ages is wrapped up in one word—<u>service</u>

—first to God and then to mankind and then to self.

"Why do you let this tree get so tall?" asked New World Educator. "Don't you know, that isn't an equitable arrangement for the shrubs."

If you keep on shaking out your pig bank soon you will have only a sow's ear left.

"Why're you digging that water well there, in the hard clay?" the farmer asked.

"Why not?" replied his neighbor. "Since you've dammed the creek I have to subvert your source."

A man caught in a blizzard is no worse than a worn an trapped in a bad marriage. All of nature conspires to destroy them both.

The teacher who neglects her office to discipline will soon find her class torn into tatters. She must then expend twice the effort of instruction to draw them together again.

"I hold here in my hand the key to your very salvation," said the cleric.

"However—you don't know where the lock is hidden," his student quipped.—from the play "Absolution," by Fa Le May

Let no man become the master of your conduct lest you become the slave to his will. In due time he will; attempt that purposes

Among your elixirs of truth and knowledge, keep none that will poison the well of honest enquiry.

Have you never put the right shoe on your left foot? Then why do you berate your friend for his error?

Be careful of a lean and hungry hound. It may be his masters distemper and not the dog's appetite that has mad e him so.

There is no place on this earth better adapted to a man's natural belligerance than the house of his termagent wife.

Since there is a price on every thoughtful deed, there is a cost to being penurious—friends.

I once owned a horse with a wooden leg that was filled with the jewels of a Russian countess. You may logically ask how this came about. Logically, you will not get an answer.

Grifter Foe Fum sold oats by the sack. In each he cut a hole, excusing the dribble as an open seam in the burlap, Clever merchant, he doubled his interest on the debts owe d by collecting the spilled oats for resale.

Pull down the defense of your strength and you invite predators. The tree weakened by age attracted beetles, the cropland depleted by overuse relented to the dust story, t he lion crippled by a thorn *in* its paw attracted man's gun, the nation rotted by corruption invites exploitation., This i s a law of life.

As you grow older you will attract self-appointed executioners intent upon belittling your years and quenching your joy in living. Turn them away like the dirty beggars they are. Scorn to listen to their meek invitations to e an u i and quitting. Know that they are the defeatists of earlier years.

I cannot understand the rag of indifference wrapped around the eyes of justice. Ought they not to be seeing eyes with vision, compassion and acceptance in them?—not sightless eyes but visionary eyes, not eyes blind to the scales o f justice but discerning of the reasons for the balance?

Patiently, one log after another, the woodcutter split hi s cord of oak. Little did he consider the work involved but only the ends of warmth and comfort. Like him ought you to govern your thoughts and order your feelings, to t he ends of wisdom and understanding.

An umbrella on a clearing day is the sign of prudence. When the gods thunder for obedience the birds fly away.

The feral animal will feed from a kind hand. There is a certain animal wisdom in its submissiveness as it sets a lately renewed old nature aside.

"As soon as the log left my hands and crashed into the flames and embers, i realized I could never create but only enjoy. I am therefore to be pitied above all men, since I am neither a hedonist nor a libertarian."—Anonymous

Many discuss relationships; few understand their complexities. They can be full of perjuries, doubts and false accolates and yet survive, intact.

Quarrels over money dislodge secret dislikes in marital affairs. Yet why ought money to spring the lock to the cage.

A young man's cavalier attitude toward money is less fashionable than it once was,, He now feels only the constraints of his own purse.

Let not the mouse of prodigality invade your house le s t it become his by eminent domain.

Wisdom without a sound premise of right or wrong is like a kite flown in a high wind without string. It flies willy-nilly and is destined to crash without purpose.

The evil in men's hearts is endemic else the world would be getting better.

"Take your hands off a me or my daddy will blaze a new trail in your thoughts!"

—Marsella in J. W. Longtree's "Tonsilitis," a farce a-bout young love. (Act)

Roll over and flatten down an honest compliment with protests of fake modesty and see if your carpet of friends. love doesn't wear threadbare after a while.

Would a hungry man steal food to satisfy his pride?

The reason the other shoe didn't hit the floor in the room above was because he had a wooden leg. Some folks just don't think.

Do you hide the Good Way from those who follow lest they curse your footsteps for deceit?

Keep your debtors waiting and your creditors may attend the funeral of all your fine promises.

It is better to assume you have little talent for an onerous task than to inflate your ego with presumptuous . gifts.

Do not feed the goose to fatten the gander but let each kernal of <u>will</u> be thrown to its necessary purpose.

If you stop to bandy with the viper and the fox. you will pick up their ways of venemous attack and clever deception.

Do not let the mockingbird of envy shape your song for you. You were created to unique as to sing a special melody. Search for it, find it. play upon it. Thus will your day s and your ways come alive and your song will be especially yours.

—from "The Philosopher, Trudgin." A Song.

Hold fast to desire since it is the force of wisdom a *n* d errs only in misdirection. Death is the cessation of all desire, all appetites.

"I'll not give in to his insults. He carries his pride like a lampstand in the wind and I intend to blow out h is little flame with the puff of trutb."

—from "Journey Alone," (III), spoken by Lawyer Grouth, in a play by Henry Claxton.

"How can you just stand there and complain about my muffins? They are basically my mother's muffins, and if you attack them you attack my mothers Oh, I see the litigious possibilities in this."

—Christian in "The Shadow," a murder mystery by playright Ted Forsooth (Act I, ii).

The feral dog is more vicious than the coyote since it attacks on two levels of perception: wild and domestic ate d. Each potentiates the other.

Close your mouth or you'll catch a fly. Open your mouth if you would be heard. Life is full of ambivalences.

"How can you be so unkind to me who gave you my virginit y and my life and yet asked nothing of you?"

—Smolena in "The Travesty on the High Wire," a serious dram a by Lup is Larsen (II, iv).

"All of life is a glorious whirlagig that never quest i on s the motives of the players but demands all that they possess."

—Bill Struthers, as Clown in "Circus Tent," (III, ii).

"To trip the light fantastic, dearie, you must have clearly in mind what is—fantastic. What is debonaire endures. What is false falls to the floor of its own—clumsiness."

—Maxie in "The Instructress," a one-act comedy.

"Do you wish to keep the dictators waiting on your decision, Mister President—or shall I ask them to proceed on their own cognizance to bomb the helpless?"

—from "The President's Report," a drama of extremes b y Gertrude Oberamergau (Act II, i)

To countenance evil continually is like accepting a gift from hell as grace. There can be no compromise; the jest is that Christians have.

Upon the rim of the wagon turns the vision of the journey. Pierce the nose of the beast and fix retribution.

A man will sacrifice all that he possesses for the love of a beautiful woman. There's a community of exchange there, for both are perishables.

If the way is hot, exhausting, take a little rest. The journey can't be all that urgent, since life seldom is.

As a quiet voice of reason cannot be heard in the tumult of violence and madness, so a song cannot be heard amid disharmony. Hell tries to conjure up both conditions.)

The lion escapes its enclosure by the sentimentality of a meddler.

The devil choses his victims not by their weaknesses but by their strengths left unguarded.

Curry favor with the rich and you indulge their problems. Immerse your life with the poor and you share their raiseries.

Do you search for a purpose in life? Then hitch your dreams to the skills that are yours by nature. *Do* you fancy that God is a prodigal?

Only a fool will challenge the fury of a hurricane yet ignore the commandments of the maker of both.

When the wind moves the branches of the tree to scrape against the side of your house, do not look for tree squirrels. Have a just appreciation of causes and forces.

If the effect is the result of the cause, then the search for causes begs the question of certainty. Without c e rritude as to a cause or causes, they do not exist except in the mind alone, for a cause cannot be proved before it exists and being non-existent defies proof.

—from SOPHISTRIES, by A. Quagmire, Conundrum Publishers.

To the rich man the beggar is an enigma. To the ragman the scion is a result. Their commonality is their i improvidence,,

Hang onto the hats of convention since they secure the hairpieces of your respectability.

—by Piquance from "Old Ivy Magazine" (Boston, 1897)

Judge a case, hypothecate justice.

If you run around with lions you'll begin to act like one.

An adulterous people are leaderless.

A pious man is like a ravenous beast who roams about looking for someone he can inflict his piety upon.

Do not scorn the simple pleasure of the old swimming hole. It has few replacements in today's artificial lifestyle.

The preacher dipped into his pocket for a rag to wipe his tears away— and found there the undelivered eggs of his sermon notes.

Kill the bottle and murder the brain.

Wine is impervious to the pious voice of censure. It takes an act of the hand to set down the cup.

Most of life's problems have their source in laziness for which money is the chief prod. God is the other.

Fat chance, skinny opportunity.

A sad tune whistled off key is due to ennui. Both can be amended by practice.

Despair is the misbegotten progeny of untimely cynicism and unremedied failures.

Despair is an attitude, like some folks don't like catfish. Either can be corrected.

The length of a mile is an arbitrary human distance. Why not allow God to arbitrate human harmony?

Retirement sucks. Thus spake Zarathrust, a busy person. Lose a penny, squander a doLiar.

The best way to save money is to do like the farmer does to his winter potatoes; he saves them.

If drugs are such warming, relaxing, buzz imbibings, as one judge described them, why are they not distrubuted among prisoners to encourage the acceptance of their surroundings?

She plowed into a snow bank and came up thinking of marriage.

A disturbing thought is like the crash of glass from a broken window that cannot be repaired without effort.

An unkind word can bore into a man's soul like a heated gimlet. Forgiveness will arrest the damage but not the pain.

The lodestone of discontent is the magnet for irresponsibility.

Do not see-saw with a sluggard or you will find yourself doing most of the work.

Play is the natural bent of the human mind whereas work is not. Therefore, convert your work into play a n d your play will produce the fruit of work.

I lay there at night and listened to the patter of little feet across the floor. Then I remembered I had forgotten to set the mouse traps.

I'm told my baby sister was cradled in a dresser drawer to protect her against the draft and the rats. In that waterfront town the rats and drafts abound.

If you would fly with the eagles you must risk that first adventure.

Like a duck flying too low, an easy thought is sure t o wind up on the professor's intellectual plate.

Hypocrisy is a disease endemic among Christians, not be cause they know no better but because they doubt the integrity of their critics' wisdom.

Practice piety and worship hypocrisy is you'd succeed a s a churchman.

Secular hypocrisy bears the stamp of fraud, religious hypocrisy puts on the face of kindness.

Pride is like a house upon a ridge that violates nature' s profile. It stands out only because it is usually offensive.

Always keep one hand free to contend against the spoilers.

Love never converts to hate or indifference without residual memories.

He who blows out all the candles save one has a flame b y which to light his way. Observe the iconoclast.

Americans, strangely for a hardy people, believe they are entitled to their luxuries. The source of this notion is religious. A righteous man (with God) always deserve s more than he has.

A sinking ship is no place to count your dollars.

"If thou spendist more than thou earnest, what profit i s there in loss? Or—rather, dost thou find pleasure in thy pain? There is a certain pathos to the joy therein, me thinks."—quote from an anonymous Country Squire, 1779 (Tombstone)

A dictator's soldiers are less to be feared than are his policies of suppression.

Crack a tyrant open like a clam and you will find therein the poison of his season.

America's national debt is like a black hole in space, an incalculable waste of dead energy impenetrable by law.

Sow a little, reap a lot is the principle of a good investment.

Cheap thoughts and irresponsible opinions tend to run in packs, like feral dogs.

Beware of the scales whose balance is sluggish to t h e touch.

Mock a champion and win a following.

Hidden malice in another is like a concealed dagger.

Scraps are for dogs, fishwives and seagulls. Let all communication be done with calm.

A scuttle of coal is worth a pound of medicine.

Pot pie is rarely one cook's invention, like a convivial household,.

Listen. Before the knock of opportunity you will hear it s approaching footsteps.

The maxim that "silence is golden" begs the question of when and where. Answering these may transmute silence into lead.

I used to write in the sand for God to read. Now that I am grown, I write on rock for men to see.

A child rarely gets enough of swinging. So ought it to be in our desire to do good, were we but children.

An icon worshipped for the real thing is a pagan form o r animism.

Seize upon it, claim it as yours—a piece of the "t r u e cross," And—taste of immortality for a moment..

Termitic wood will emit a hollow sound, to be distinguished from that of a musical instrument . Not all people's ears are so reliable.

The quintessential maggot will turn into a fly and go about its contamination as always. The quintessential lie is much the same.

A staircase ends somewhere. Do not let your purpose in life be so vague.

That low moan can be the wind or a dying man. Life will teach you which.

Experience is everything in religion nowadays. I me an, if you experience a sensation of flight out of your ʀeligiosity it must be so. Have faith and— take off.

The ice heaved and groaned like a bent saw. There is always a time for flight.

Push a little, pull a little and you get nowhere. Be war y of objectors to your favorite projects.

"Cancel the order."

"Why, sir?" "They haven.' t paid for last month's shipment."

"But, sir, they are special." "Specialty has its limits, Modgrum."

"Yes, sir."

—from THE PIATFORM OF NIGHT, a 5-hour trilogy deali*mg* with monetary dilemma. First produced <u>Embassy</u>, Wash., DoC.

A chimney in want of repairs is like a disposition in want of attention. It endangers the entire house with the threat of fire.

He who believes in witches endorses witches, one of the black arts of Washington politics. Witchcraft is the deux <u>exmachina</u> of the liberals.

Mow the metes and bounds of your opinions lest you trespass on the exact knowledge of your neighbor.

Revenge is ingratitude set to violence.

How can I rest assured when I have no possibility to 1ie down on?

An impregnable argument, like a cowl of snow, settled down over the snowy hair, eyeglasses and bony frame of the baffled professor.

Call the dog to his bone if you would test his hunger this may be applied to any unfulfilled need of promiscuous enterprise.

A wall whose stones are missing or broken is like the will of a person destroyed by hardships.

The runner who's always comparing his speed with his competitor's will lose the race by default..

No matter how fast your horse can run there's always one that runs faster. In this way look at the achievements of your life.

An argument that does not resolve itself is like a knee out of joint. It goes nowhere.

A wish unmet is like a hole dug without seed. A keen mind is kept so by constant use.

No matter how you cut it, the heart of a wrong will always reveal an injustice.

The antidote to the poison of slander is the balm of truth.

An ambition blatently thwarted by jealous men may sputter yet never go out, so long as the coals of memory are left.

Let no man wear your hat lest he wear your image also<>

The pleasant tinkle of ice in a tin pitcher of water is much like the laughter of the frivolous mind over subjects of grave concern.

Thank your benefactor while he lives or you may rue t h e change in ownership.

Listen to the crickets on a warm summer night. Do they not teach you that happiness is often found in discord.

A man who will drive a wagon with three wheels demonstrates an irreproachable faith in the dynamics of gravity and skill.

"If you drive them cows too hard, mister, you'll wind up with only skin and bones at the railhead." Anonymous"

A secret lie is no better than an open profanity. It is better that neither is given utterance.-

Try to call a coyote with a whistle. Some persons will never be domesticated.

A person continually afflicted with bad debts is a leper to his creditors.

Certain critics have likened Washington politics to a merry-go-round. A whirl-a-gig would be my contraption cof choice, utilizing windy Congressmen to cause the President to chop wood, or the members of his cabinet to appear and disappear at unmarked intervals.

Think of the imeasurable energy and courage it took to carve this country out of the winderness. And thencon sider the cultural junkies of today—one worlderswhoput us down.

The huckster with a shoddy product to sell is out of synch with the forces of synergistic flow. His dishonesty will eventually trip him up.

Walk a little, rest a little,, You'll eventually get there.

A man married to the wrong woman—or vice versa—is like an actor on the stage. His lines after a while sound scripted and his deceits predictable.

Said the hub to the spokes, "How many you are." Said the spokes to the hub, "How singular you are." Said the rim to both, "Though I surround you alii as one, we need each other."

A pitch in the roof is like one's calm words in a storm .They divert the rains of criticism and sconi.

He who wants no depth to his life is like the thin man who gets lost in the cracks. He has the appearances of being real without the substance.

A woman without a mate is often scorned when young, chastened in middle age and pitied when old. Who should really give a damn?

A wayward son is less like a ship without a rudder than he is a cloud in the current of the wind. Most often he goes not willy-nilly but directly to the cause of his peril.

A diamond in the rough—who knoweth it but the expert ? Then make thou no pretense to its discovery.

He who is weary, let him rest. He who is young, let him play. He who is dead, let him lie. The only final alternative is work. Let all men pursueit.

The looks of a thing are all that matter to some people. You will find their minds, like their houses, cluttered wit h furniture, dust-gathering and bargain-priced.

The fires of hell are not for man to stoke with human souls. Guard against spiritual presumptions.

Defeat, once accepted and then again, becomes like a well-worn hat, comfortable.

To bring in the government in order to cure the criminal of his disease is an insidious act of naivete.

A child who plays at war games is less likely to become a killer than he will a saint, an instinctive revulsion and a merciful God directing him thereto.

A trail blazed by a pioneer is soon forgotten while that bloodied by a criminal is remembered forever. Does this not speak to man's natural depravity?

If Jack tumbled down the hill with a pail of water—he had no business running.

Hang a man from the rafter of his own house and you've created a skeptic of him.

A child yearns to be an adult through sex, violence and imitation. Ask yourself in what ways they advance maturity.

If there's too much government in the lives of the people, they'll run for cover in hard times.

A person with a double mind claims that he gropes for a n equitable answer, whereas he in fact possesses no evidence for either side.

To say that one gives a rap for the troubles of another person is to describe a small effort.

Live and death are the apogee and perigee of life. Experience is the orbit and the human condition is the energy. Go for the ride.

Triumph and defeat are discreetly separable. To believe anything else is sheer nonsense.

Always remember that satan commands the forces of darkness. Do not trivialize his capacity to strategize.

Some folks' minds are like a gate that bangs is the wind. They cannot latch onto a solid idea.

As the wheel turns. so doth the grain grind.

If you would capture the enemy you must first think like the enemy.

Every stone in a rock wall has its significant purposean d would be missed if removed.

Have pity on the waif of the streets. for who knowsbut that Providence will! accord you a similar measure of misfortune.

The broken spirit of a man is like a fence unmended. Challenge the cry of the wild and—become savage.

Living with a spendthrift is Like rowing in a leaky boat . Every month you've got to bail out the debts. Every so often you're swamped, and there never is any real security.

A natural kind of politeness is now on display in the pale-ontological section of the museum.

Do not be cruel. At least rattle before you strike.

The expedient measure is sometimes doomed to failure. Would you prop up a sagging roof with a hoe handle?

A good intention that fails is like a coffin without a bottom. Of what use is it?

Do not make a compact with the devil or he will let you lead his parade.

No lock is safe from a desperate thief,,

Jealousy will motivate only in the company of a legitimate ambition. You must team them up together.

Loss of faith in another person is lake a leaky vessel that will eventually sink from mistrust.

Two men who bargain for the same horse will rarely part friends.

Show me an example of a man who is truly humble and I will show you one who loves opportunity, which forever casts its shadow before hint.

Like two magpies that quarrel over one berry, envy most often afflicts those who have little to offer of a kind.

Would you be a contemporary fop? They affect the dress and manners of the corporate image.

Celebacy—who wants to play priest for the remainder o f his life?

Malevolence walks in the same footsteps every time.

"Women and children only! Woman and children only! Sir, are you a woman?"

"I feel more like a child at this point." "There's no disputing you're a man. Then lie like one. Women and children only."

—from "The Sinking of the Ship <u>Sonorus</u>," by Bartie Taylor

Pity is like a rescue by an avalanche cord. If you wait too long with actual help the victim will die from the cold.

Sugar to a horse does not feed the animal; it only bond s you to its affection. Thus is unmerited sympathy to a questionable friend.

Remove your shoes to show respect for the tradition. Once inside things will go easier.

"Keep up,the good work, sergeant. Scatter your men." "Sir, they're already scattered—some won't never regroup."

—from SGT MAVERICK, a movie

Some folks say the loss of memory is a terrible thing, I say the loss of a friend is a much worse calamity.

To cripple enthusians effectively, you must first strike at the root interest. Then the passion to progress will face—and you will've achieved your insidious end.

The big, brave man pulled out his pistol and shot the little squirrel to prove his manliness . It's too bad that such stupidity goes unrewarded.

Like an argument, a leg of lamb can be prepared in several ways.

"That was a strenuous vision," said the ancient philos other to his cousin, the astrologer.

"And how so—what do you mean by 'strenuous'?" "I mean, simply, that it was so far-fetched I had to exert every effort to believe in it."

"Then next, I shall relate to you my convenient vision." "And what is that, 0 astrologer?"

"That God is all around us,"

—from the <u>Harlequins of Faith</u>, by B. W. Dexter, AAN. SOD, DDD.

-4-

Humility is when a sourdough don't tell nobody he's struck it rich until he puts on a shine down in town.

A tolerance for the unique is a sharing with God.

Would you be courteous to swine? Then why do you ask forgiveness so often?

Most vulgar men are contented with themselves. The offense others take merely amuses them.

Good folks called her "cheap," yet it was their attitude that was cheap—easy to come by and not costing a dime.

The best benefactor to a town is a dead murderer. The n he deals rightly with the body.

A handshake that merely pumps water draws little respect.

"A dead man is the only sober man in this here town, sheriff o"—anonymous

"You leave the Diety to the Tribunal of heaven, y'hear? They got more money up there to prove His case."—anony.

If you brag about your nugget you'll only cut in the cheats and thieves.

Better a live bait than a dead lure.

Once escaped from the lips of a man, his words can no longer be hammered into shape.

"The mark of the beast"—what is that but the absence o f intelligence in its widest sense?

Condemnation is an act of the law—otherwise it is arrogance.

At the summit of the mountain there rest. All else is struggle .

"Conform!" commanded the god of chance, wishing to protect his territory.

Keep your purse strings tied if your nature is prodigal .

The night of poverty will eventually fall over the lazy one.

The Senate Whip is the bellwether sheep to the entire Congress. Ever notice how he escapes through the trapdoor after the delousing?

Debt is like a constantly ringing bell. Silence its clapper by paying your creditors.

The value of an acre of ground or a cord of wood is not s o much its size as it is the utility. An acre in the desert and a cord of cactus do little good to anyone.

Wealth:—what is it but human energy materialized?

Be liberal if you would not be prodigal. You can oft e n justify the former but rarely the latter.

Credit is the expenditure of what does not exist—Hike a n unlit Log in the hearth.

Debt and poverty are cousins. The trick is to keep them separate.

A sullen child is like a canary that mopes. Surely there is a remedy for its silence.

Envy is the attack of the ego on the soul. Its cure is achievement.

Better a thimblefull of hope than a barrelfull of wishes.

We all have vanity but some of us, like being too fatare burdened with its excess.

Vanity is the counterweight to insecurity.

The wife who only ornaments a marriage values herself very little—as does her husband.

Can you remember tomorrow? Then it is equally as abs u rd to recover the paste

Leave revenge to the criminal. How else can he respond?

The fact that flattery is a human foible ought not to deflect the honest compliment.

Leave warfare to the ignorant—except for the defense, for no aggressor ever foresaw the calamities precipitated by his attacks

Test the waters of controversy with a question before you plunge in.

Thy parents ought to be thy chieftest source of values in this life. All around is conflict and chaos and the limitations imposed by your young experience.

A forgiven offense is like a forgotten jewel, yet do not try to recover it or it loses its value.

Confess your transgressions into the wind and earn nature's indifference. Confess them to man and win his disdain.

Bear a tale, carry a stone.

A rebuke to his teacher is a shame to the students

A person who thinks knowledge can be acquired without effort would level all mountains.

To strike a fire of commitment in the heart of a man absorbed in himself is like trying to start a fire with wet wood.

The shipbuilder did not design his vessel to entertain the craftsmen. Hew to the line.

Wave the flag of freedom—and express what millions are yearning for.

Honor is the heart of a person's integrity. Compromise it and you subvert your house.

Cop a credit—and become a fraud.

If you've reached the bight end of the rescue rope and hang suspended—pray.

"Her hair? Well. Have you ever seen a burning Bush on top of a plain desert floor?"

—from "Plainview," the magazine for women.

Pride, one of the seven deadly sins, is an adamant taskmaster It demands constant attention for its maintenance.

The misanthrope lives in a house without doors. The bite of a lawyer can kill.

A good man will atone many times for his imaginary wrongs; an evil man will exploit them as unmerited grace.

A penny's worth of candy is no remedy for hunger. nor is a faint compliment a satisfaction for accomplishment.

Flaunt your wealth if you'd invite the thief to steal from you.

The point of an argument is seldom lost in the questions it raises but rather in the answers it elicits.

Whet the appetite. sharpen the pleasure.

The gold and the punishment ought to balance on the scales of justice.

Big noise, petty cause.

The trap set upon the trail makes use of old habits. Let the snare suit the weakness.

Ingratitude is a clock that does not work. There's no accounting for future benefits.

Building a road means felling trees. Only a horseman can get around the problem.

Hold the mule, ignore the fire.

"Keep your wits about you, Cleghorn. The snakes will take great pride in investigating you."

"I know what I know, sir."

—from HENCEFORTH, a discursive drama on the sins of merriment.

Peaceful is the night's rest pillowed on a Smith & Wesson revolver.

The best preacher of God is in touch with his diggings. With the harvest of gold come the tares of envy.

File a claim in heaven with God if you'd know where you stand.

Greed and possession are natural conspirators. Thank a swindler. win an enemy.

Revenge belongs to the zealots. Be careful or else you will join the wrong gang.

The sound of distant thunder warns of rain. Ought we not to listen to the distant thunder of human discontent?

"A little discourtesy is much admired these days, Mister Pit."

"I be not so discourteous as forgetful. and I won't tell a soul, Toodles. You'll soon be popular."

—from THE SCANDAL OF DALLIANCE, By Horace La Monte. A British film.

It's a pathetic fallacy that the willow weeps, though I have heard trees that moan in the wind or drip cold tears of rain.

If you take a rogue to court be sure his lawyer will find you out.

The major difference between a politician and a states man is that the politician will salt your mine without a n y qualms; the statesman experiences discomfort in doing so.

In the early West the six shooter beat the jack of diaraonds with a royal flush. Nowadays the IRS holds t h e trigger hand.

The pride of a man gives him the motive to roar.

We've heard much about the "insensitive" person. Why ought the other party to demand a sensitive response?

Steal a loaf, got to jail. Steal a nation, become a shrine. How paradoxical the British sometimes were.

The wealth of a nation resides in its liberation of opportunity—a process rather than an accumulation,.

Salvage what you can from the wreckage. You williat least have a symbol for your losses<.

The illumined mind is not always the most experienced. It is frequently the one most discerning—of values, priorities, conducts

Skating on ice that cracks is like pitching an argument that fails.

Listen to the rocks of failure fall into space if you would know the depth of the canyon of defeats

The mind is faster than the maching—or must we endure another tyrant?

Suspicion in the mind of a woman produces a failure in confidence that rarely if ever recovers.

The sluggard always leaves his slimy track—like his relative the snail. For each it is its singular accomplishment.

The chart and the compass to the mariner are like the Wisdom Books and ambition to the sojourner.

Jealousy is the mismanagement of the fool. Is the ant jealous of the honey bee. or the termite of the woodpecker. All are diggers.

Kick a dog and you kill a friendship.

If you live on a windy hill, expect the wind to blow.

The last thing a man with a big mouth wants is a small listener.

Nine times out of ten the faulty law is an expedient law.

The bigger the noise, the more oracular the speech, And humankind will listen to the loudest voice.

The gull circled and landed on the dead fish I had cast aside. How wonderfully does nature provide!

Sow no love, reap no friends.

The vane of time fixes the perplexity of deceit to the moment .

An owl. in a pine is no better off than an owl in a barn-except for its game.

Modern man embraces the power of his machine and the machine his power. In ancient times he shared this intimacy with nature.

Do not verate the shef for burning the roast. After all, you can eat squab.

"Do not put on the sepulchral face," said the elder to his parishoner. "Your serious countenance does not fool God.,"

The size of the wheel is not as important as its forward momentum.

All men yearn to be treated fairly. Most do not abide.

Give me a ruble and I'll tell you how much your worth, for by the manner of giving you reveal yourself anonymous

The thorns of the rose insure its survival. Too easily seized, too readily destroyed.

Rock in your chair to agitate your old thoughts.

The character of the wood will determine its splitability.

A man's nature at birth is much like grapes on the vine, with a capacity for turning into either wine or vinegar.

"I would never sell my diamond ring," said the matron as she slipped it off her finger for her lover.

The grasshopper is too lowly to care about the appetite of the king.

Loose thoughts are like leaves in the wind. Chance will settle their patterns and colors.

A life without a plan is like a voyage without a charting.

Listen to the mockingbird. What marvelous variations" Liken your life to this.

I'll considered thoughts must soon melit away like new snow under the warming sun.

A dulled conscience in human affairs, like a rusty weathervane, is of little value.

Happiness is like a welcome friend who never intrudes but is always present.

The genesis of much crime is self-pity. Even the leopard can open a sore in its flesh by constant licking.

A man who is excessively proud of himself dresses infeathers that may smother his heart.

A dog that barks incessantly is a satisfaction to its owner but a vexation to a thief.

Troubles kept hidden inside are like a bunged-up bar r el of sour wine.

Do not ask a person to turn over a new leaf unless you are familiar with his horticulture.

A welfare government inspires ingratitude among the people.

To catch a fish, you must learn to think like a fish.

A friend long waited for is like an oasis. He giveth rest to the spirit, comfort to the bones, and refreshment to the eyes.

You'll never catch a wife if you hang around philanderers. Better is independence than questionable fraternity.

The libertine is tolerated today as a Father Counsel lor to the young.

Reason without common sense makes a stepchild of experience.

A dollar saved is a dollar confiscated—by the government. No tribunal is complete without the Judge of Compassion. Asceticism is the refuge of the indolent and the fakes.

An opportunity will often come disguised as work—yet also as unnecessary play. Be discerning.

Of the squandering of the leaders and the indulgences of the people, intemperance ultimately fastens the stocks a-round freedom.

"Headsman. let the axe fall."

"Aye, sir—a good souvenir for his majesty comin' up."—from "The King's Counsellors" by James Ji. J. Wilson, III

Honor is a characteristic that can never be transferred but only lost.

-5-

The radio has become the tribunal of life. Its laws are hearsay, its shamans purveyors of narcissism, its counsel the words of canards and fatlings. Society is indulged.

Cater to the libertine, embrace his paramour. Then crow like a cock if you would lay an egg.

Do not keep a philanderer waiting if you enjoy his attentions, since you may not live to enjoy his money.

A dream rounded out in awakened reality is still a dream, defined.

Pity is the insignia of the sadist and the Christian alike. Know which side you stand on.

The servile man protects his pride—though he often b e-comes the tyrant when released.

Flattery is the hinge between corruption and accomplishment.

A woman's beauty is sacrificial. a man's sacramental.

Forgiveness belongs to Saints and Angels. Do not try t o fake it.

Unmerited ridicule can break the wheel of progress. Be wary.

A derelict barn is a sad thing because it speaks of an industry now gone.

Wax the saw if the wood is wet. Wax your speech with humor if it sticks in their craw.

Trifle with a woman's affections and you invite her scorn.

Sing for a meal and you may be asked to stay and play f or the banquet.

Envy is the trademark of either indolence or incompetence.

Poor joinery is a compromise in accuracy. So it is in argument and in art.

The message of all calamities is:: Exercise care at all times. Be sober in all things—if you would be right.

Acquit a criminal who is patently wrong and you jeer a t justice.

It is sorcery for a nation to bind its productive citizens by non-productive laws in order to affect leadership.

A marriage of interests. temperaments and experiences is like a well-fitted joint of timbers. There is strength in the juxtapositions-of grain.

Be sober in wreaking justice. After all. the laws were not fabricated in a wine vat.

Civil disobedience is a rebuke to a corrupt authority or a perverse law.

Train up a hawk and it will return to its master. Train up a child and it will fly from its parents.

The vice of today's society resides in the secular piety of excessive forgiveness. Ext It is good to treat corruption as the voice of reason and heresy as the expression of Self.

You cannot bake a pie without heat. Why do you try to concoct a drama without passion?

Cherish old ways not because they are old but because they are proven good and wholesome.

Greet teenagers with sobriety for one of them may be testing your heart.

A government that imposes its will autonomously is no longer of the people. by the people and for the people.

Wit is the ability to see in a different light.

Often the more strenuous the goal! of accomplishment;, the more objectionable it is.

Fine a man for his wrongdoing and you curry his dislike of authority. Fine him without cause and you incite his distrust.

Esteem the great, belittle the humble. There is an ugly yet consistent attitude throughout.

"Death with Dignity" honors satan. It acquiesces to the sting that remains.

Germinal ideas rarely spring into full flower upon a first hearing.

Put no price on integrity, for it cannot be bought.

Hatred is the soul of satan's wisdom and violence the passion of hell.

Treason merits death or exile. What else remains?

Murders without the sentences of just retribution ought to wind up your conscience against the justice of rogues.

When you hear their triggers cock in unison your final ac t on this earth ought to be a prayer since the irial is beyond debate.

Religious music glorifies both God and the church. Man's participation is almost irrelevant.

Diligent practice more than intelligence marks the achieving student.

Cultivate friends if you would harvest their praise. Fragrant flowers, musky weeds. Some prefer the latter. Criticism, justly weighed. can be a boon to the connoisseur. Ridicule is the license of fools. Reflecting upon old mistakes brings on a weariness.

Fashion is but the amusement of the indulgent. What price indulgence!

Distant crags invite distant thoughts. So ought vision to be.

Countenance a fool and you cheapen your understanding.

Capture a love—and you may be compelled to release it later.

Art premises man's enjoyment of his creative nature.

Taste ought not to be a discardable but rather ought to rest upon standards which endure .

A citadel is a defensible place. That ought to be the wall of honor encircling a man.

Solemnity walketh on quiet feet. So, too, ought reverence.

Wealth is not just the product of labor but of superior d ensign.

Why feed discontent with the errors of another? Let each bear his or her own in sobriety and strength.

A good carpenter keeps his tools sharp. So, too, ought a craftsman in the arts by diligent study and practice.

"We've drawn up C Company on the flank, sir." "Good, Then all you've got to do is to hole."

"Sir, my men are ready—eager..."

"A holding action is every bit as necessary as a thrusting action is this strategy, Lieutenant."

—from THE RUN OF THE BLOODHOUNDS, by A. J. Simpson, Brig. Gen. (ret.)

Just as the REWARD poster was shot up full of holes, there is a certain evidence of culpability in any crime that is inescapable.

Philandering is the province of the wealthy and their e x-pensive laws. There is a double standard there. What does it matter who gets the money— the whore or the pimp?

The Environmentalists would purge and cleanse the planet of offensive men. How very much like God they are beginning to act.

Like a weak argument or the spirit of defeat, a canoe in a stiff wind will slew in the direction of least resistance.

Other women imitated the beauty of her Looks. The beauty in her voice they could not.

The insolent man builds only a mud house with his insults.

"Why should I remember any of your damned kindnesses, Regina?"

"Curse them if you must. I intended them for your own good when I gave them out." "Then you've retracted them."

"I've retracted nothing, Charles, except my goodness toward you."

—from THE SEMINOLD COMPLAINT, by Capt. Ormsby of Frt Ramsdale

Doing things in a different way was an old American tradition. How sad—conformity!

When you think you've reached the end of your rope—tie another one on.

Better a loud bark than a small bite.

Do not be in a hurry for the elevator. The bottom of the shaft will always be there.

Mine for gold. settle for trouble.

Remember this, that a ministering angel answers to his employer.

If you take for granted old friendships, just remember that all things in this world move toward decay.

Grow apace if you would look upon the king's banquet. After all a short stature comprehends little.

High in the mountains in the wilderness. I understood that life was Mind.

Eat an apple, discourage the worms.

Test your Christian friend to see if he will forgive you for your trespass. Scale his wall and pound on his door with out entry. You have but proved the ugly side of piety.

The law that warns the stranger not to break the close puts a value on property.

Tolerate a little scraping away Q-f thy treasure and, anon, thy treasure will be revealed to robbers.

If you stub your toe you will thwart your will.

Respect the man who breaks his bread. He often eschews the dainty and fastidious mannerisms of the effete.

"Under the influence" is like skating on thin ice. If it cracks and you fall in then you will know by the difference in sensation.

If fast to itch, be slow to scratch.

She wears clothes like the skin of an onion. What's underneath would make you cry your eyes out.

He has a disposition like an unpainted house. All the defects and bare spots show.

Cheat the poor and curse God.

Half the battle in competition is in looking like a competitor.

A measured beat, whether of music or a man's way in life, can be a dull pace.

A yea-sayer is a rebuff to the misanthrope, for whom <u>n o</u> is his curse.

Confiscating money and property from the people is as sweet and easy as purloining their <u>bon bons</u>.

Would you bargain for a horse with bad teeth? Then why negotiate for a house in decay?

Neither the keystone, capstone nor cornerstone has the same significance in life as the milestone.

Don't be a dinosaur. Adapt.

Time may be the river but the springs and freshets are the wasted moments.

The caw of the crow is the voice of insistence.

A logger without a forest is like a nomad without a desert. Neither will survive for very long.

If you're a mule, don't act like a filly. Spring the trap and squander the pelt.

Measure your savings as carefully as you measure your spending and your house will have a floor in it.

Thy lips are like—like—a No. 5 Crayon.

"Close the window," said the invalid to his servant. "I don't want to catch my death of gold."

Master a craft, avoid beggary.

The horse's bit was not intended to torture the animal but to communicate the will of the rider. Thus ought every law to possess a spirit in its application.

Kick a horse, ride a mule.

There are easier ways to amuse the crowd for money than to chase the greased pig of entertainment.

Let no one impugn your honor end get away with it. That is an acceptable intolerance.

The porkbarrel, repository for the makings of soft soap and axle grease, lives on in American politics.

Raise your hancll There's no way all can talk at once. The lowly button may save the President's appearances.

Some people's minds are like tinkling wind chimes that summon the wind and little else.

Shuffle the deck and confuse the enemy. Satan is not privy to your thoughts.

Passion is the energy of interest.

Pitiless the execution, devoid the understanding.

Call the hogs—and stop a revolution for hunger.

There is a power of evil on the loose in today's world. It's identification is chaos, pain, dissension and d estruction. It has no specific embodiment perceivable b y our senses. But the results it produces are distinguishable from their opposites. It shed light in such a way that the rays are defracted and misleading,. Its sweet ness is poisonous, its satisfactions are evenescent and chimerical. Its voice cajoles, seduces with empty promises to need human needs, real and imaginary. Avoid it. For the pain of your sacrifices will be small by comparison with its torments.

Vintage care, vintage wine.

"Lend me a dime," said the panhandler.

"If I lend it to you I'll have to charge interest." "What about a gift?"

"What! And be in your debt. No way."

—from THE MODERN CONSENSUS, by Homeless Cloe, itinerant playright.

May the ruts of the pioneers' wagon wheels remains W h a t makes modern electronics so noble and memorable?

A self-centered person, like a rusty weathervane, is of n o value in showing the winds of prophesy.

He was a leader who wound up the clock of time and perpetuated history. He caused events to happen.

Authority is power,, There can be no quarrel with this premise.

One word of gossip can destroy a library of achievement.

Motherhood is Biblically right, rqcially acceptable, biologically harmonious, culturally consistent and almost universally respected. So what's the big hangup?

While you are throwing caution to the winds, would yotil, mind throwing the results also.

Accept a bribe, nurture corruption. Count your pennies, squander your wishes.

Retribution — how little do judges nowadays understand its significance.

A much-considered problem produces a confusion of advice Deceit—snare its source and understand its fictions He is a dull man who listens to no others than himself. Beg for a candle, owe for the light.

A man who says he has never lied is a walking specimen o t the truth.

Bullshit used to be the specialty of politicians but now preachers engage in the exercise. Is there a fundamental difference?

Hang up your fiddle and your bow if you must, but don't neglect to dance.

Do not praise another too copiously for his edifice of life hath hidden flaws.

Sin is not a culture trait; it is universal. Kiss a cow and sensitize your neughbors.

A disease caused by promiscuous conduct cannot be explained away, since viruses, like bullets, issue from a gun.

Covet thy neighbor's wife and gain a bed in hell.

Avarice, if practiced long enough, will quicken the hand and still the heart.

The law was not intended to punish; its purpose is to ccntrol harmful conduct.

Gluttony, one of the seven deadly sins, requires dedication in its rites to the god of consumption.

Sing no requiem for a lost cause. It had its day i n court.

A confiscatory government will enevitably leech upon a productive people.

Fell a tree, foster a stump. Some things leave little behind.

The composer establishes the key to his music as a de terrent to chaos.

A board that is true is a pleasure to the carpenter. So, too, is a good wife.

Chase a thought, capture a quandry.

Abstinence will purge the scourge of promiscuity.

The libertine is tolerated today because onone likes to feel guilty about his or her conduct.

The magnet that attracts also repels. This is much like Hedonism.

He who claims he has experienced God enjoins satan.

When the owl blinks the image of its wisdom flies.

It is not the length of the line that lures the fish but the kind of bait.

Mechanical modern man intrudes upon nature. The Xndianat one time killed the sacramental deer when the pursuer suffocated it with Rollen. The Anglo invades life with his gun and his machine. They interpose. They falsify supremacy. They enshrine the attitude of arrogance. They destroy union.

Splitting wood is like splitting responsibility. Both pieces of the log burn faster and give off greater heat in the endeavor.

That we can put a man on the moon is a technological feat of the times. But restoring an ethical and moral basis to a corrupt society is an accomplishment for the ages.

Ar. you planning a deathshead bliow to evil? Then soak your axehead in the water of reflection overnight lest you lose your advantage.

A wry smile, a gentle touch, a new understanding.

Are your thoughts lofty? Then provide a latter of logic so that others might reach your level of understanding.

His life is wasted who never gives a moment's happiness to another.

"A penny for your thoughts," said the vagabond to the politician.

"And why just a penny?" the old bear asked. "Why, sir, because the weight of your thoughts willl fet c h little more."

—from "The Tin Cup," a play about debauchery, dishonor, profligacy and all sorts and manners of moral abandonment in the Congress.

Would you emulate your neighbor? Then his decisions govern your life.

Inherent genetic deficiencies do more to extinguish a species than does the spoilation of mankind.

A politician is like a ripe plum for the appropriate lobbyistf. The lobbyist is a loaded trap for the right pelitieian.

There is a thin line of trail that exhilarates, far above the reach of others, whose journey thereon draws upon stamina, curiosity and anticipation. It is the trail of new discovery.

Few people like a loser; fewer still can identify with him.

"Fire in the hole!" cried the powder monkey. who then sought cover from the rain of rocks. How like the activist without a plan.

Guilt in some folks makes them feel either impowered or a-neraic. In the former guilt fuels charisma, in the latter it sucks blood.

He who scoffs at the law doth scoff at other things as well.

Pocket the difference if it is yours, otherwise you claim ownership of your dishonesty.

Self-indulgence is the bonding of alii sycophancy. Wicked deception curries benign favor.

The steam engine will say, "I will do what I like with m y power," yet it must follow the rails. How very much like it is the rigid traditionalist.

Sacred lives are fitly preserved when ordinary lives are oft discarded. In each of us there's a simple juris prudence that creates reverence and disdain.

Do not berate the children so for their noise. Remove the toys of adults from their possession is you'd hear bedlam.

Many a village was begun, waiting for friends to arrive. A child's jealousy is instinctive, a man's foreshadowed.

Were the worship of God a science,, all the world w o u Id be on its knees.

The success of a scientific experiment is not so much i n the outcome as it is in the denouement—what folHows.

Strangely, God gives His creatures puffs of air by wh i c h they inflate themselvest the puff-adder, the puff-lizard, the puff-parakeet, the puff-lawyer . Inevitably the puffing instills fear in the enemy.

If you'd change the road signs to misdirect the ignorant, how much easier it is to change the guideposts of moral laws to misguide the naive.

The hard jolt of the wagon in a gopher hole broke the axle. Do not let a disappointment in life break your hope or progress.

As the lawyer chewed and whittled on his pleading, his adversary of cause cut to the heart of the wood with a clean blow of the axe:. Wrong is never a matter of accident but of choice, never amorai but unethical, never of a b sent conscience but of present evil intent.

Why doth the man of means oft avel at a poor man's w ay, the measure of his water well, the thrust of his spa d e? He fancies his dominion is the quintessence of success, and in thinking thus he faces failure.

The blind man feels his way along? Why ought not the philosopher to do the same?

Instant repairs are usually haphazard, as often are hasty replies.

He who overloads his scow with the projects in life ought not to be surprised with water over the gunwales.

The cloven hooves of the Satyr often mark the surly man. s way.

Cut to the line. Do not saw beyond the end of the board in debating issues or you will fan the air of ridicule.

Foreign investment in America, what is it but envy translated into money.

Essau's birthright is America's Judeo-Christian heritage. Stuff from abroad has become our lentil soup.

Take the right fork in the road—and be pleased with what you discover.

Sportsmanship and sports are dissimilar. The one involves fair play, the other cheating and deception.

Satan thought more highly of himself than he ought. In his great beauty he exchewed his Creator and sought par it y, Many men do likewise nowadays.

Rock the boat, cradle disaster.

To learn of a man you must cultivate his friendship. To destroy him you must exploit his weaknesses.

To mock a man you must parody his strengths; to laud hi m you must extol his virtues.

Free food is worth no more than the thanks of its reciever. Give liberally only if there is a corresponding gnaritirtude.

Remove your improvements upon nature before you assault the cutters of trees.

"Clean out those jackals with a raking fire, Lieutenant and don't spare the bullets."

"Yes, sir. We've all got a investment here."

—from a closing scene in "Timely Interlude," a drama about WW I, by Cassidy Welch.

"Why do you swing your trunk so?" the little man asked the huge elephant.

"I swing my trunk to entice your stingy handouts. If I did not loom so large you would ignore me."

—annonymous. In a like manner charity must impress its donors.

Vice is legalized in a corrupt society,, This is the tolerance that is accorded depravity, for which religion becomes a curse.

"You haven't got a whistle of a chance of getting through that mine field, Sergeant."

"Not chance I'm looking for, sir." "Better keep moving—dont even stop to think."

"I'll be too dead to think if I set off a mine, sir."

—from "The Flowering of Hell" by Sanborn and Wilson, play-rights.

A man without a purpose in life, a direction, is like a windmill that has stopped working. Even strong advice and the directions of experience fail to draw water.

A notiched gun is as worthless as a notched stick, since murder accomplishes nothing but waste.

Intelligence in small forms of life is instinctive behavior. not cognition. Therefore man's cerebration ought to be described as conduct.

Row a little, rest a little and the current will prevail.

Look at life as if it were comprehensible, then you can at least attribute your mistakes to human error and not to capricious chance.

A government whose leaders are ideologically blind will produce stupid laws and chaos. Leadership requires vision,

"Me first," rattled the mindless stone, threatening to crush onward.

'Give way if you can," gravity replied. "He intends to use me to destroy."—anonymous

Look at the lines in a man's face. Do they appear ugly to you? Perhaps he is reflecting back your soule

Largesse toward other men is not a matter of quantum meaj-surement but rather of doubt as to the response.

Doth a man build his house without a roof? Then why tax his honesty by accusing him of thrift?

One loose chimney stone can burn down the house. So too can a loose tongue burn down a man's reputation.

You poison a man's well by watching his wife, making o f him a cuckold and of her a whore.

Stop, bathe yourself beneath the enveloping waterfalls, and then go on your way refreshed.

Plagarism is destructive for by it you are saying he does not merit your recognition of his existence.

Do not put on the mask of animism by stealing from another.

"Listen, my son—wishful thinking is like a fall from a high ledge. Both end in disaster."

A fire lit but without fuel is like love without feeding and tending. Both will die from the want of care.

Solitude is a good thing when combined with a purpose. Otherwise it is loneliness.

"I never knew the man—I never saw the man before in my life—I certainly never talked to the man."

"Then you've obviously been subpoened to witness as no witness for no one."

—from Act II of FAMOUS LAST *WORDS*. a little drama o f courtroom fraudulence and intrigue, by Ellis Wickersham.

The joy of a campfire is intensified by the dismal character of the day.

A low score in golf can be explained. a high score is an act of fate.

The fantasy archytype of the pioneer arose from the smoke of hardship, death, raw courage and hidden despair.

Old roads left untraveled grow the weeds of abandonment. Friendships are much the same.

Be wary of the shortcuts in life. They are frequently death traps.

He who would destroy civilization must first destroy the family.

A great society cannot be either preserved or raised upon a foundation of perversion and bastardy.

A judge who ignores precedent settled the law upon shifting sands.

The canons of ritualized religion almost never go off nowadays because they are mounted upon the same parapet as hell's.

"The cries from the abyss waken my nights with pain." said the preacher.

"Good entertainment is what you lack—not atonement," said the clown, clapping his hands.

—from discovered dialogue in the diary of Julium Sterne, a 15th century preacher.

The horizon of a young woman's life is too often fixed on marriage— which is more a state of mind than it is a progress of form, more ably the confession than a sinister regret, more the heritage of smothered hopes than of fathered realities.

"Sing me a sweet song of your love, my darling and I'll capture it in plastic—for the world to see."

—translated from a song of 20th century America

"Go forth," said the Anchorite to his protege, "and remake the world into man's image."

"Dear Professor—men are so different. How can this be done?" "Borrow, my son," said the sage old man.

"If I borrow I must repay."

"Consider what you borrow—sharing. That is entirely ethical and offends no one."

"Truly thy wisdom is visionary, 0 Anchorite."

—from "My Days in the Anchorite's Cave," by Chandu

Claim jumping and plagarism—there's little to distinguish them but sophistications

Our return to our roots honors neither God nor man but the precepts we once learned.

A patient without hope is a mere body before science.

Why does any man struggle to remain defeated?—yet there are those who cherish failure.

Men's yearning for peace is like a summons of pain in the night.

When dawn comes and all are asleep, why trouble ye wit h the night now flown?

A heritage oft spoken but rarely set down is most of all bequeathals to be cherished—either in pain or gladness

—for words spoken though not writ are evanescent and cry out.

Touching. it is said, hastens healing. Thus is sympathy more often an act than a word.

Few men with any regard for posterity chasten the unborn.

In the wisdom of the mountain lives the rulership of nature.

Live your life as if it counted, for if you don't you may ultimately get your wish.

A drug has two essential purposes: religious and curative regardless of how one describes the effects.

To keep the peace you must keep your word.

Well-intentioned help could botch the job. Do not let emotions enter the formulae

To enjoy living you must learn to enjoy yourself. Other men are too changeable for such an overture.

Frequent the palace *m* or the oval room—if you would ape the king's ways. Be assured that he will kindle your regrets if you overstay.

No man likes a poor imitation of himself. Why do you try?

No matter how great the achievement, small men will! detract from the effort.

A moment of surmise can lead to a labor of the years. Distruct that Christian who borrows on God's grace.

She lay like a lizard on a rock, converting her soft flesh into tough hide.

Wit and wisdom are often conjoined. Yet caprice lacks wisdom and philosophy lacks wit. When then the marriage?

The pragmaticm of American politics would astonish the ancient philosophers for whom reason was antecedent t o vision and logic the handmaiden of right conduct.

The birds hopped and tweeted in the avary. Little did they know I was critiquing their music.

A game of guns has replaced a game of marbles on the school ground. It is beneath boys to grovel in the dirt;; instead they must play in the blood like grown men.

Three visions of Pergatory moved the poet to describe them the loss of his soul, the transitory nature of life and the suffering of his alienation from God.

Pitch the ill-humor from your heart into *the* bottomless cistern of heaven's forgiveness and watch it vanish from sight.

Love: every man thinks he can describe it but in quantity, by human count. few truly experience it. It is too sacrificial for most of mankind to endure.

The loss of the bald eagle from sight. high above the canyon, was due to his indifference to your gazing. In a like manner ought a good deed to fly from you.

Lift up your eyes but in so doing ready your feet for the far journey .

Peer pressure is not exclusive to the child. Were t h is not so the Congress would have no Party Whip.

Some men are miscast. They would rather gamble away the farm than admit they have no desire for farming.

Great minds feed an small discoveries. like a whale its plankton.

Like children swinging on their ropes beneath the heavy oak tree. so are men like they who covet not the world but God's grace, for it doth give them joy and support and community.

Curry favor with a dishonest person and you dabble in deceit.

There is an instinctive understanding of the enemy in all animals. Mankind is the only creature who invites the enemy into his den. Thus doth reason create its own delusions.

A pound of trust outweighs an ounce of suspicion.

Do not go to the *Seer* with your quandry unless you'd indulge in the fraud of hell.

Throw away a friend and you value none but yourself.

If you spread your richess before strangers, surely a. thief will steal from you. Hide what you treasure, exhibit what you demean to keep your losses small.

A clandestine Love is worth more than an open hat redo Yet neither merits the justice of God's grace.

Honesty is not the exclusive possession of a judge far from it! Honesty belongs to the righteousness of God, yet who hath it but Him?

A hike into the hills brings solace from grief. Covet thy neighbor's wealth, eschew his integrity. Marry a wench, espouse a hell.

Take the small. Lest compliment you've enjoyed—"My, your buttons are shiny!" The motive was pure, yet the smaller the compliment the more suspect it is.

If you are troubled by the apparent ease of other men's gains, know first how they were gotten. With labor hath he prospered.

Keep to the upper road of honor. Avoid the quagmire o f trickeries and deception^

Love fractures readily when allowed to become too cold.

A man's acts of deception will inevitably reveal his heart.

If a boy goes to school and there learns to participate in wrong, do not his parents have the right to redirect his learning?

A pebble dropped into a tank of water reverberates against the steel sides. Thus have small things great intensity of repercussion and power of effect.

Cop a plea, bury a crime.

If you're a snake remember your hole. If you're a man, remember your cave. If you're a god remember your pedestal.

Not hatred but indiffernce is the antithesis of live. A wall begins with the first brick.

Big Government will take over the rights of parents on the assumption that Washington bureaucrats are competent t o raise their progeny. This is choice arrogance—that a bureaucrat 3000 miles distant should control the bedroom, the dinner table and the study desk.

Destroy the jury, destroy justice.

Tame the wilderness and you will destroy mankind.

The socialism of our bureaucratic state is an engrafted adulteration of the people's will. Historically! American government has always been locale

A reason countered is an argument rebuked.

Hedonism is a closed system of self-satisfactions. Mention God or purity and you will see.

As gravity is a scientific absolute, is is moral conduct an absolute. Anarchy, defiance, total autonomy hath consequences.

All of life is <u>moral</u>. Even a-morality is a moral choice to abstain from preferences when, paradoxically, one is already made.

Shoot down the pidgeon, tropy your day.

The sightless fish in the Carlsbad Caves—why do they need light? Is not man somewhat the same when he swims in the subterranean darkness of his wicked ways?

Latch the gate, unlatch friendship.

Know what it is that you fish for in life and throw your sinker into the depths of the sea.

The manners of your dog reveal the character of your ternper.

Study the law if you would think yourself educated.

Let the spirit of gratitude pave the way to your good fortune.

Tears rolled down the cheeks of the acteess as she wrong out the heart of her paramour. She loved not his soul but his body.

Stuck iii the mud, blind the way.

Fruit that falls before it is ripe inevitably rots.

Gossip is the unhinged revelations of a confidante. T h e tales will harm, but in the telling there is great sat is-faction.

A horse with gold teeth goes riderless.

The sadistic gesture will inhibit confidence. So, too, will the benign pleading forestall retribution.

A library of knowledge is not worth a covenant with wisdom.

Do not keep the executioner waitiing. For him one head is as good as another, one excuse as valid as the next, one pleading as lawful as the following. His axe will s e v er your argument from its body of knowledge.

Lose a friend, gain a debt.

Prison used to be an excuse for judicial incompetence. Now it is an excuse for sentimental forgiveness.

Try, try beyond success. There is in the effort a surety.

A mind gifted in baubles seldom comes to earth.

Stake a claim, garnish the earth.

The seigeworks of a fugitive are his murders.

The man who limps rarely runs for greed.

Wind up the clock and you'll remain punctual. Let it run down and your day vanisheth.

Honor the debt, credit the future.

Keep thy chariot running and thy chariot will carry thee.

Slander doth walk about nowadays licking its pink tong u e and baring its fangs for even the most innocent.

Collecting stuff for our comfort is addictive. Thus there is a certain confession and penitence in garage sales that translates as "need."

The lie has no defense but the truth; yet who will defend such a one?

The mud dauber and the honey bee build hexagonal nests. How perfect is instinct, for combs tolerate no was t e d space and integrate strength. Would that man's engineering were as efficient!

Point the finger, preclude the humility.

Your enemies are less likely to doubt you in your pr i d e, which they share, than for your achievements, which they do not.

Clasp what is dear to thy heart. All men are entitled to their personal treasures.

Keep cool, merit praise. Lose your head, earn censure. If thou art a pawn, speak to the player of thy miseries.

Sometimes the best scheme is to try a little and gain a lot instead of the reverse.

Privileged conversation is not matter for public exposure. The scions of the liberal media find this abhorrent.

When the bases are loaded and the call is two strikes an d three balls, it is no time to measure the spectators.

"I've not heard such tripe as condolences for the prisoner nowadays."

"It's all the rage, you know, sir—feeling sorry for the murderer and thief."

"I 4are say. Well, wait until they've shot up the crown and stolen the king's jewels."

"Sir, the Americans have given the—push—to this comedy."

"So they have—'twas a major cause of their little revolution—condolences, indeed!"—from THE HISTORY OF BERNICE, by J. J. Ludlow

A faithful employee is better than a faithless wife. Whistle for a bird and capture a song.

Cancel a debt, groom an admirer.

On a sinking ship gamblers roll last.

Know the value of money, that is consumes not of its own accord.

Ultimately one's own education, in its entirety, is his responsibility. Too much government tends to curb initiative.

If you must punish a child interject learning. I once lost my recess privilege but learned the times-table profoundly well.

When left to the power hungry and the self-seeking, the quality of education deteriorates in direct proportion to their control.

Proud men will boast of the inconceivable. Humble men will admit of the impossible . The first will seldom make t h e effort; the latter will try and often succeed.

The silence that hangs upon the tongue of a cautious person is circumspect and valued.

A soul without a faith is like a door without a latch. To protect your crops you must threaten the spoilers. A jillion pardons are not worth one simple thanks.

Keep your windows open if you like the fresh air of diverse opinion,, After all, your house is yours to adjust.

Trust the hawk to return to its trainer, as a rending word returns to its speaker.

Covet the gift of another and you deny your own uniqueness. Matriarchy is anathema to a patriarchal justice.

The measure of a man's spiritual insight is the measure o f God's honor of righteousness.

Expose a man's weaknesses to public ridicule if you would destroy the man.

Pull up a radish, season the speech.

Silence maketh a fool to seem wise.

The clothesline knows the weight it must bear. So ought well-chosen words.

A serious answer to a trivial question levels the value of both.

The man who. combs his hair backwards seldom confronts his forebearers.

-6-

Frame a lie but utter it not and you have earned esteem by your silence.

He who splashes in iniquity soils his facade.

"Lis'n, Ca$'n, few men wot's kept a count of his—les call it—his spiritual life—ever lived one—livin' in the spirit is not like keepin' track of your horsy bets or yerartil'ry pieces, Cap'n, It's way down inside wot's important ."

—from Act 3 of "The Major Calamity of Sheffield," by Clare-mont Foster, Esqu.

Silver is one thing in the hands of a craftsman and quite another in the hands of a thief.

A tongue that wags brings teeth that bite.

He who eats rice with his fingers can govern his mouth.

Would you give away your richess—your porcelains, jewelry, and precious metals? Why then dost thou give away thy honor to acquire these things.

Put no food into the sun of adverse criticism lest you spoil its flavor.

The censorious word when undeserved oft brings pain that is undeserved. Foreknowledge begs the issue.

Three miles walked is still one less than the next.

Kill a goose, feast a prince. Feed the gander, fatten the spies.

A tall man and a short lady have in common their discrepancies.

A child without counsel is a stray without an owner, for who will care for it?

Bless the wedding with your presence. That ought to b e gift enough.

The heart of a person may fill with tears while in the belly there is laughter.

A thousand miles, like a sore foot, will kill the de sire to walk.

Accept the good gift from the good with grace. From the poisonous one, reject all good gifts.

Hang onto your temper lest it inspire the irrational deed .r word.

While canoeing down the river I saw the spray envelop the rock. In moments of crisis one's sense of direction b e-comes acute and critical to steerage.

Keep the peace, addle the discontented.

Over the lip of the rapid we poured, like a chunk of butter in the milk. Compatibility with the turbulence was everything.

One leg over a horse is hardly an excuse to ride away.

The wasp tarantula preserves the former's larvae. Who could have worked out this miniscule problem in logistics?

Hurry the turtle, stampede the rabbit.

No man will sacrifice what he loves without enquiring the cost of the exchange.

To make a clean breast of a bad situation, bathe daily in forgiveness.

A crow that caws is more selfish than an eagle that screams.

Bolted doors make solid walls. In a crisis do not be quick to find the breech lest thou give egress to the enemy.

Large numbers of people make intimate conversation difficult. Small numbers make public address impossible.

The barking dog acquits itself for its presence.

The laborer who will not work ought to be handicapped sin c e grace to him is expensive.

The rhinestone has replaced the pearl of great price in worldly minds.

Danger comes to all folks at some time in life. Why ought the government to recreate the womb?

Discoveries lie off the trail, confirmations upon it.

A poisonous cup can kill. So, too, can a poisonous accusation

He who beats his horse deserves his own justice,, the retribution of the animale

Salvage the best of a poor situation by claiming extenuating circumstances. These are like the nails raked from the firing of the barn.

A sorrowing heart is blind to joy. Curse the night. glory in the dawn.

The value of a football player is 200 times that of a school teacher. Society sets the comparative worth of these entities.

To crush the will destroys the stamina.

Do not change your wigs simply to please your husband or to amuse your friends. A wig is an exercise in fashion and a rebuke to nature.

Throw away fortune. embrace endeavor.

There are some who climb the ladder of success without hands others without feet and still others without brains. T he first two are dexterous. the last is an oddity.

Prove no losses, measure no gains.

I have no quarrel with the party's platform—only in the shoddy way it was constructed.

The windswept plain did not recognize the vertical man.

He possessed a conical brain to fit his conical hat, broad at the base and sharp as an icicle at the top with little but air space in between.

Take no for an answer only when <u>yes</u> would fail of results.

The epistolary manner of his delivery frightened even the church mice.

Cue the action, you begin the scene .-

Time and the currents of opposition will surely alter the course of one's life. Make allowance for these factors in planning a career.

The arbiter of morality is often a participant in immorality.

Attrition of purpose brings the surrender of will. One drifts and wanders without the navigation of purpose.

When the harlequin smiled a thousand others grinned.

Care for your child or the Government will preempt your duty to do so.

Pretense is less offensive than is knowing arrogance.

The laws of man are God-annointed only when they attempt to carry out His will. What is this nonsense about yielding to Nero and kneeling to Hitier?

The well-built house had generational value.

A monopoly is less to be feared than is a stringently controlled competition. The one owns a hedgemony but the other inspires devious acts.

A patient man is rarely a sorry man.

Lost men seldom returned from the Badlands—not because they were bad and banished but because they were lost. 'Tis much like life.

A beautiful melody is worth far more than a cacophony o f noise. Listen to the songbird.

It was the lowly hotdog that gave birth to baseball, notthe other way around. Feed the crowd if you'd regale the day.

The black bear does not retrace its tracks. Usually its carnage is wreaked upon first entry.

Judge the crime,, condemn the offense.

"Let us share and share alike." said the rider on the carrousel's wooden horse.

Query the stranger. ignore the journey.

Take marriage seriously but do not destroy it by an excess of sobriety.

In human relationships a teaspoon of honey is worth a pound of salt.

"You must learn. my son. to confront the world head-on." said the Anchorite. thumbing through his parchments.

A fire on the hearth cannot melt the ice on the doorlatch.

I had a student once who read the encyclopedia for amusement. He tested moron. Do not confuse a person's reading material; with his brain capacity.

High on the mountains the granite crags await God's fine.

Information is of little value without insight into its applications. No? Then commit the telephone book to memory.

Fly. if thou believest in space, for no visible law deter s thee, but if gravity should seize thy flesh and bean t h ee earthward, thouwit then believe in absolutes.

Learning becomes virtually a dry waterhole when teacher jgoower supersedes subject power.

Injury done to another is reckless, to thyself lamentable.

Taxes without representation led to the Revolution for rights. Today taxes with representation has led to a revolution for power.

Defrock authority, enshrine chaos.

Leave the taxes to the tax collector. Why ought you to share in his calumny?

Learn to separate the illusion from the reality.

Draw poker requires only the labor of lifting oneshan do It is a game for dullards and the indolent.

Kindness belongs both to the rich and to the wise. Why ought mamon to divide the spoils of goodness for himself?

Throw chance away, you will still invite speculation.

Haste not only makes waste—as the old saying goes. It also makes a pauper of courtesy.

A soldier on guard is of greater value to the army than is a general in his bunk.

Walk slowly along the journey to your destination, for speed merely churneth up the dust and obscureth the signposts.

The wedding feast shares joy with strangers.

Just as wicked men slander a righteous God, so do wicked men defame a righteous government. For how else doth corruption take hold?

Tasty food begs no diners.

The well: born man hath Little concourse with gypsies. This was Hitler's appeal to Germanic snobbery

The stakeholder ought to be neutral but seldom is. After all, his service fee betrays his participation in the contest.

Survey the cause lest your options close.,

The halter is for the groom, the bridle for the rider. Know thou the difference in thy projects.

Stitch up thy lips if thou'd keep thy speech seemly.

Trust the way of the worm. Though it is blind it sees with its flesh far betrer than eyes. Value your instincts along the blackest roads in life.

Labor without effort achieves nothing. Effort without regrets accomplishes everything.

Like crossing a railroad track. allow little time for partying under hazardous conditions.

Mend thy boots or walk in the mud. It's alii a matter o f choice.

A fitting epitaph remembers the grieving more than it does the departed.

Poverty deadens the pain of commiserate care<. Pride quickens the spirit of a boastful reply.

A small; flame of is great potential to a visionary.

Some poor slob pays fifteen dolilars to watch his favorite player earn a quarter of a million. The disparity is irrelevant to his enjoyment.

Is it not better to reemburse the victim's family with the same money used to support the commuted lifetime prisoner? The retribution would be just.

Praise a little, envy a lot.

A sweet perfume is a challenge to her competitors, a sweet speech to her suitor.

It isn't the facts <u>perse</u> but how one uses the facts that distinguishes an educated person.

If the morrow is lost in the night, how ought one to calculate the passage of years?

The artist with integrity will not hide behind novelty.

A cave is no less a cave when a habitation. A house is n o less a house when a home.

Polish thy speech and win with charm; polish thy boots and win with force.

Imprisoned for a belief, exonerated for a crime …

We hear much nowadays about "gut reactions" to deplor able circumstances. Yet these Seers are often thin persons t o whom <u>gut</u> is foreign and <u>reactions</u> are choleric.

The muzzle-loading rifle had this in common with its Colonial revolutionaries—the king's stuffing secured a deadly blast of reprisal.

As hail destroys a crop of corn, so public disapproval ca n destroy a wisdom perspective.

The steam caliipe once thrilled the crowd at the fair with its silvery magic of sound. It was the common man's pipe organ, the answer to Europe's cathedrals amid the elephant dust and bigtop canvas. Worship has had many voices.

"Samuel, do not cry that they're putting your father into the ground."

"But, sir, what if he air still alive?"

"Oh, goodness ne, now—you'd hear'm—bells aringing, him pounding on the sides of that box he he were."

"I think I hear'm now, sir.,."

"Them's the spadefulls of dirt they be trowing on top o f that box,"

—from dialogue in *HIS* HONOR, THE BELLRINGER, by Harry Trumpet of Allswythe Lane, London. (People once feared burial-alive and supplied the corpse with such instruments. Ed.)

Trifle with a bear if you'd fight for a cause.

"Death with dignity" is a euphemism for prescripted murder.

Treasure what things others hold dear. You may inherit them.

Barbarism—how visible it is in our indifference t o war d life!

Blasphemy is the equivalent of a prayer to satan.

Stumble on a rock and measure yout length. That's one way to gain ground in either a debate or a stroll.

If you call it quits you're sure to double your losses, once for what is past and once again for what might have been.

If you would live longer than most, you must think life and not death, for in the very thinking comes survivals

A dish prepared in haste need not be sumptuous, only tasty as hasty pudding and cornbread.

Were the victim to retaliate for his death, he could let his irreversible retribution proceed upon the evidenae.

Education for all persons is neither a right nor a privilege. It is a necessity for a nation"s survival.

Mortify the flesh and you condemn your Maker. Beggar your education, barter the future. Keep no secrets, carry no grudges.

Misconduct In the classroom destroys the education of man-y who would learn.

Education is the creative world of the minds of others made made accessible to honest enquiry.

The fox in the chase is to the hunter with the horn what a goal in life is to the improvident. Once captured it's all over.

Discipline seldom deters action except when the res. Its seek to expunge the discipline.

The bait in the snare is the truth about appetite. A mind gifted in baubles seldom. tsdown to earth.

"Why do you get into such a big argument over your hammer? Doesn't the nail get driven just the same? Then pound it in with a rock if that'll make you happier."—from "The Framers" a short comedy by Jasper Felspar.

Fruit that falls before it is ripe inevitably rots.

Tell your innermost secrets if you'd invite a caravan o f the curious. Remember. however, that once begun regrets are too late.

By diligent and prolonged work, the average will surpas s the superior. The journey is the test.

If you march to the beat of a different drummer. learn *his* refrains as welli.

The catafalque of political wisdom is where the Government exceeds the people's will.

The triumph of a feeble effort raises no claims to greatness. The failure of a great effort surrenders no claims to defeat.

Lead a free people to the brink of war and you will bury their trust.

He who boats down the river will surely walk back.

As a rabbit leapeth to avoid the pursuing hound so ought a man to fly from sordid gain.

The man of faith is a man of stamina.

Purity is less a condition of faultlessness than it is of motive . Think about this.

Do not swear unless thou wouldst cast thy soul upon the rocks.

As interpreters of life, artists are among the guarantor s of civilization. Being guarantors they ought to affiirm life.

Ours is today a culture whose cult is the Theism of THING. Technology is our panacea and our pleasures are Dyonesian ecstacies revitalized. The efficacy of THING has replace d God, and that is superstitious animism.

If men hate one another they revert to the dogmatism of the Middle Ages, for the fierce hostility of the dogmatic is the product of ignorant fear.

The artist must acknowledge the potential and real humanity of all mankind—otherwise human beings become artifacts of physical paleontology.

Chain the conscience of the individual and you outlaw taboos through punishment and social exile.

The journalist invites men to understand themselves through news events.

To get an education is the process of always being ready to absorb new insights, new knowledge and perplexities.

A nationneeds men and women who can think in the abstract, since a government cannot be run only by mechanics.

Hardship rarely begs to be heard since its evidence shows on the sly.

The silence of a long journey weds time to distance without comment.

Higher education ought not to be the parvenu of the snob but, instead, the plateau for vision developments

Sloth speaks not so much of a man's laziness as his failure of interest.

The terrorist lives in a world of visionary delusion that he can permanently change the status quo by force.

Since career jurists are so by the people's vote, their rulings are frequently suspect of mollifying leverage forces.

A well-educated man can move in many circles. for his mind has been opened to other views.

Education is a respecter of persons—those who desire to learn. It merely tolerates the others.

Education premises that the history of a nation deserves to be transmitted to succeeding generations. A people's ignorance of their history augers the return to their primitive condition.

An education gotten easily is of little value to the student. Disdainfully, he will treat it as either trivial or useless. These sorts ought not to go beyond common schooling.

A good teacher cannot force the student to learn. She often works against cultural ennui and social lag.

Old mistakes are better left dead. Let not their lessons cloy at memory.

Know this. that your enemies will not love you for your default but for their plunder. Thus did God motivate the Jews to collect their Egyptian swag.

In a tug-of-war. the power blocs being relatively equal.

it is the footwork that wins the contest. So it is in diplomacy .

Make an anchor of time, waste the substance of effort.

Do you wish to see the mystery of God's love for beauty? Look into the depths of the sea—or into a good woman's heart,.

Collect all thy marbles of promise if thou wouldst break the ring of confidences..

The Epiphany of the saints parallels the weariness of the damned.

The delinquency of the parents usually gives rise to t h e delinquency of the children.

Conventions are puerile and empty when only duty motivates. Service the want,, esteem the reply. Though speech vanishes, the pen remains. Feed your jealousy, starve your integrity.

It is better to cultivate the friendship of an enemy t h an to sacrifice a thousand armies to the doubt of hostilities.

Privacy defended is privacy exposed.

Trust the court only to the extent of the evidence for acquittal.

Try harder if you would succeed at failure. There is a small: satisfaction in the result, at least.

Lawyers have earned their lamentable reputation because of their commendable greed.

A pound of forgiveness is worth a ton of rancor.

Hold no man captive of his word if there is evidence that releases him.

Sweat—what is that nowadays but the evidence of a disease. Addiction to the truth is the chalice of the wise.

Plant at the wrong time and your seed is wasted. Thus it is with hasty promises.

A stranger more trustworthy than a brother rarely petitions for redress of a grievance.

A poor student will excuse his sloth; a good student will admit to poor preparation.

A man inherits, the State confiscates and God adjudicates.

Parents will often protect their lazy children and so d e-fend their own disinterest.

Bread and water for the prisoner will quicken his appetite for freedom.

The more we protect the imdifferent in the classroom t h e less we can expect from their performance. Why cultivate laziness?

Preserve the ballast. save the ship.

A sweet song is not always an appeal to love. It can be an enticement to death.

The schoollteacher who cannot rule with words must carry a whip for his donkeys.

Repentance makes anew the connection between God and man.

Marry a woman with a dowry and you marry pride. Marry one without a coat and you mate with penury.

A gentle breeze of encouragement will fill the most s e nsitive canvas.

Fire and fear are an ancient unity. Thus ought passion and conviction to profer the same thrust toward the enemy.

Doth the woodpecker complain because of his humdrum job? His survival lies in his labors of provision.

If fire purges and water cleanses, then doth not air revive? Carry a tune. bury a song.

The latitude of a man's reason ought never to transect the zero longitude of persuasion or he will stand speechless.

Survey the cause before your options close.

There is a piety that tyrannizes over the conscience. It s direction is censorship.

Concocted circumstances will often belie one's integrity.

To learn, one must endure the tension between knowing and not knowing. The acquisition of understanding re m o v e s the pain—temporarily.

From the apathy of the people arise the abuses of powen. Political cynicism is the dryrot of the body politic.

A low voter turnout imputes fraud and manipulation to the contestants.

Any court that silences objections to its forgiving attitude courts favor with the criminalo Judicial impotence arises therefrom.

The view of mankind as a pragmatically functional reagent to uncontrollable forces is fatal to his survival.

-7-

Respect the convictions of other men even if you disagree. Were they silent you would be less well-informed.

Borrow a lot. steal much more.

Remorse is the pang of inaction at a time of need.

The nomad is a contradiction as a neighbor. So, too, is the hermit.

Jump when the occasion warrants joy. otherwise you reveal your imbecility.

Traffic in drugs and you will parley in hell. The end is the result of the means.

Know a little, talk a lot.

Silence is the best antidote to ignorance. Keep thy hand in thy pocket and thy speech contained.

To keep order in your house. keep order in your authority.

A thousand gnats that buzz around one's head are no worse than a thousand confusions that hum within.

Oppressive laws will destroy initiative in a free society, for its citizens are accustomed to self-sufficiency.

He who patronizes lust is perfidious in hope, for the one begs instant gratification while the other will defer.

A broken axle can be an omen of defeat.

In a contemplated suicide, the will to survive can be like solid ice that slowly melts away in the emptiness.

Tarry at the crossroads and learn of men's choices.

The harbinger of justice sometimes occurs as a mute voice of warnimg.

Trust in an ex-convict and ruin a thief.

Few know that the chicken gave rise to the egg—since God created the chicken.

Would you put your enemy to the task of burying you. Then stand clear of his enmity.

Some sorts of pride—as in achievement. craftsmanship are curative and can heal the savage wound.

Some persons are natural teachers, for they comprehend ignorance and the thrust of disinterested enquiry. They deal boldly with facts and can separate the trivial from the significant.

He who is lazy mentally will seek the lowest level of satisfaction. He will revel in the euphoria of his accomplishment.

The title of Educator is vainglorious, while his humble task is to initiate enquiry and inspire the search for understanding. Whether he fails or succeeds in his role he will take others with him.

If too proud an Educator will not share, if too acadeinic he will not produce, if too inured to the formalisms of the academy he will stagnate and stifle enquiry. And if tradition-bound he will not seek new knowledge.

An Educator ought to make humility his <u>sinequanon</u> because he stands before the world as the repository of knowledge.

A common <u>idée fixee</u> in American society is that the teach e r ought to entertain her students, since they attend school mainly to enjoy rather than to learn.

The test of a good teacher—one of them—is the intensity of interest she inspires in her students.

If you would ride with the gods you must conquer your fear of heights.

A book a year is the prescription for teachers in some universities By pacing they would control their timing.

War contains no substitute for its enemies unless is is the pretense at diplomacy. The one is dubious, the other idealized, and it is the latter that usually prevails.

Privacy defended is often privacy exposed.

The man who will milk a dry cow will distrust pragmatic reality.

Whilest scorn is an insult tendered to quench one's pride, arogance will often cure another.'s indifference.

The right of the people to defend themselves cannot be separated from the law. Welfare is not a response to endangerment.

True fantasy involves acquisition, actual or imaginary. I t often springs from lifers entrapments.

At what point and under what circumstances ought evidence of a private nature to be made public in a criminal! trial?

Crime and the retributive torture of conscience are closely related.

"Y'know. Maxie, dey's always foisting der troubles outer m e to suits their own program—you know what I mean—like tellin" me what fixin's

I gotter put twixt my bun and the other half. Y' know what I mean? Dey's busy bodies wit der deli comestibuls—sompin I cain't witstan."—Herbide, from "The Winter We all Fell in Love," the musical comedy by Pearson Harkenstrompt.

Alumni who promote sports to support "the ol' school" h a v e already denegrated their education.

Ten attitudes will prosper a university:

(1) that mental discipline is its own reason for existing; (2) that broad knowledge abets specialization; (3) that one cannot prophesy future events in order to qualify the learning; (4) that utility ought not to be the bellwether of studies; (5) t h a t sports deserve a minor place in university life; (6) that the university is not for an established elite but for the contributors to society; (7) that academic standards ought t o be kept high; (8) that smallness combined with self-sufficiency ought to rule development; (9) that not winning but playing is the more important thing; (10) that the measure of its success is society's cultural and ideological enrichment.

Ten attitudes will destroy the value of a university:(l)that it is a stepping stone for richess; (2) that is is the training ground for professional athletes; (3) that it was established primarily for the sons of the rich; (4) that all youth regardless of motivation and diligence ought to be allowed to enter; (5) that its best support comes from the government; (7) that standards ought to be kept low so as to a d-mit the greatest numbers; (8) that attendance is a right i n our democracy; (9) that its training ought to bear a one-on-one relevance to post-university life; (10) that little i s to be gained from studies in the classics, in logic, in philosophy, e tcp After all, life wilL go on.

Acquiring an education is largely the process of applying the mind and tools to the tasks at hand. W h ether the challenge is skilled debate or the building of a wall, this is true.

The teacher, unlike the mechanic, does not dismiss the students overnight. Their minds are of greater importance t o him than his own peace of mind.

Americans look at the image of the teacher, Europeans look look at his social station. The _image_ is promotional) the _station_ is iconoclastic.

Trust in truth, evaluate the circumstances, for by the unchangeable one you can change the other.

A good education beyond the common school is not merely an adornment, for hen its purpose has become tawdry, its function self-gratification and its end idolatrous.

Unsatisfied idealists are usually the "victims" of marital quandries. Their mesalliances are insurmountable, their rivalries impregnable, their losses bathetic and irrecoverable .

Capture the excesses of your generous ways with good deeds o That way they will keep until the morrow^ though times may
worsen.

Mend thy boots or walk in the mud. It's all a matter o f choice.

The best advertising is illusory and escapist.

Not all dogs are created equal. Why then should men be?

No man knows his neighbor better than the fool, since the one finds honesty to confirm his own deceit while the other is less than honest to find in the fool a neighbor.

Before feminism there was uselessness. Then, the brave struck off the chains and old roles fell away. The drudgeries and boredom relented before— street marches and rivalry and total license.

Can a piece of analytical prose seem so profoundly irrational as to excite intelligence? Consider Joyce's <u>Ulysses</u>.

The pietist, if alUowed to wreak his destruction, would reduce the non-conformist to a position of nihilistic illusion.

He who remarks that common school education is of little value considers his wealth acquired by accident o The power and wealth of a nation will decline without an educated citizenry who know their own history.

Education is the condemnation of ignorance, while it is the perpetuation of history in its broadest sense . Silence the monkeys if you would pray for peace.

Unprincipled men with great power in their hands always seek to level excellence out of fear for their survival.

The government would help where a man is born by its intrusion into lives. There is a benign tyranny to such adjustments.

A government of men, a rulership of caprice.

If the homeless were just, they'd have prepared for t heir rights by expanding on the law of adverse possession

A government of laws, a rulership of reason.

A buckle without a shoe is the mismanagement of poverty.

Do not let men with less ambition and intelligence t h a n yours govern your actions, for often they are not qualified to do so for themselves.

Doubt the talebearer and champion the truth.

Liberals in government demand that the people be controlled; the conservatives that they be set free. The one posit s stupidity and indifference and the other intelligence a nd enlightened self-interest. Obviously both believe in the bifurcation of America.

Good parenting is less a question of guiding that it is of caring. From that discrepancy issue all the solaces and bereavements of child rearing.

A government of means is not necessarily a government of results. Thus the wealthiest agencies usually seek their own welfare first—the Departments of Housing, Education, Environment and Transportation. In the first: skimoffs; in the second power plays; in the third land seizure; in the fourth pressures' through funding. Their operatives will survive!

Any agency that duplicates the work of another is a fraud against the people.

Is it not strange that the tongue of a man that can lead an army can sing a babe to sleep?

Any agency blind to its own corruption ought to be abolished.

A promise that lures the poor is poisoned with clever disdain. It usually seems benevolent; rarely is it benign.

A government that no longer respects the individual is a government no longer fit to govern.

Do not brag too loudly or you will attract the envy of the undesireables.

A government with weak leaders is discernable by its a voidance of issues vital to the people.

Gold dust in the eyes of the poor is no substitute for gold earned by their hands.

Public money that is thrown at a need is like the dog that returns to its vomit.

Curry favor with a tyrant if you'd find company with rogues.

Self-serving servants are the corrupters of good government. They conspire against the people through graft, bribery, favoritism and privilege. They are the drummers of the welfare state.

From the child springs the man. From the kan flourishes the childe

Infidelity is cruelist when either has believed in the other.

A government of laws is not the same as a government of lawful acts. The former may shield the incompetencies of the latter.

A wheel that does not roll is out of sychr. pwith its mates.

"This guy who said, .See no evil, speak no evil, hear no evil, 'how does he come out of it smelling so sweet. I mean where was he all this time? In the lab?"

—from "Blatherskyte," a Frenchified comedy by Willie Kramer, the "witch doctor" of the theatre.

The original mind is a threat to the insecure, since it comes from an unnanounced direction.

"The Idea of a University" fails to state how persuasive is custom in the scholarship of fresh minds. Academia trashes good students on a regular basis for that reason.

Man is the most territorial of all creatures. How else do you explain war?

Adultery is the <u>sine qua non</u> of the "good life" in today's America, say the Hedonists. What ever happened to just plain living?

In the theatre, its all in the doing.

In all of man's efforts to be God he fails to mimic His a t-tributes.

Politicians rarely contend for raw power; they contend for recognition for it is that and not power <u>per se</u> which ix n-sures their reign.

Foster a compliment, adopt a stepchild.

Not all power to the people is beneficial; not all benef its enjoyed by the people mandate their power.

He who takes great pains to insure his profit will customarily spare no effort to secure his survival.

Lead a people to demean their leaders and you foment distrust but lead them to praise the critics and you inspire agitatior.

A bastard child is to be lamented. Let pity be its wet nurse and the world of judgement step politely aside. Alexander HamiJLton was one such as this.

Know the cause in order to appraise the results.

The terrorist fantasizes that he will be a martyred hero. He fears the failure to become so before his comrades.

Almost all terrorism is an attempt to blackmail under t he banner of consanguinity.

It is not the Government that makes sacrifices; it is the people. For the Government can only curtail.

The pessimist is thrice victorious and once defeated in his mind.

While power may secure the peace in so doing it often threatens the war. Much of this century pivots on that premise.

Weave a web of doubts whenever falsely accused.

Power in the hands of one man if, of course, a dictatorship, yet in the hands of the majority in a democracy it is a benevolent tyranny. Usually the outcome is a choice of r e-wards.

A fool is less than a fool when he admits to his ignorance.

Power seized by a government benefits the feff. Power lawfully gained by a government benefits the many.

In the cave of doubts, mark thy way with a candle of understanding—so that thou canst return to the premise of supposition.

Curb your appetites if you'd taste of good things in this life, for gluttony doth destroy fine preferences and discrimination.

Sentence reduction is often a confession of the courts impotence, not its compassion.

In an insurance gotten through intimidation, fear retribution.

Plea bargains are like the sale of indulgences by which lawyers grow fat. This is a form of repeat trade, often assuring the lawyer of a place in the Schema.

Art—what is it but a creative statement submitted to society for their comment and enjoyment? If it disgusts, then the work is not art for it has already destroyed pleasure.

Why ought a culture to preserve a poisonous work of art for the sake of a personal pleasure? The latter does not endow art with value or the passing of a generation would extinguish the art work. Therefore, intrinsically the art must have value personally and anthropologically as "mine" and as "ours."

When you have reached the edge of the roof in shingling, know that there is no further labor required. This is like some relationships.

Believe that the government will be corrupt and by d o in g nothing you don't deserve the chance to correct that corruption. By degrees do men enchain themselves.

The power of the spirit to discard capital punishment exemplifies the tyranny of the majority, for they thus rule out restitution. Under a tyrant revenge replaces restitution., Think about this.

Art is neither created by committee nor sanctified by goveminent. What then is the test of art? Consensus? No. Vote? No. Reaction? No, propaganda? No. The basic element of art is that it enlighten and therefore art is pedagogical in the broadest sense. It communicates a perception that instructs. Resist the instruction and one condemns the perception; reject the perception and one discards the instruction.

If you would salvage lost early years, you must condense the future years.

Never rest content with the results of an election. The low turnout speaks for the majority ex <u>officio</u>.

Wanton murder generates the euphoria of false power. Barbarism stalks our streets.

Great power does not always lead to benevolent laws, just as little power often does.

Keep your willingness to yourself if you're not sure you'd join. After all, do they need your expertise?

The protectiion of the people from themselves and from outsiders is the principle function of popular government. Yet from this purpose issue the excesses of*t* confiscation, invasions of privacy, mollifications of corruption and wickedness and the manipulations of petty bureaucrats. The people will hate what they cannot control and weaken where they must be dependent.

Adopt an orphan and join hands with God.

A powerful government abuses its people by controlling their lives, a weak government by ignoring them.

Is man's grasp of life so arrogant that he can cultivate a dinasaur in a petri dish? Scientists still search for the extinct plasma.

By the vote may your will be known. By abstenance may your indifference be shown.

A cautious man is a boon to his neighbors, a noisome man an aggravation to his friends.

Stake a claim and garnish the earth.

"Only the king and God have conspired, my Lord." "There's a fit conspiracy if ever I saw one."

"Ought I to tell the Dean, my Lord?"

"The Dean! The Dean! The Dean! I thought he was found in bed with the queen's wife."

"You.have hit it, I think—sanctuary — a troublesome one nonetheless."

—from THE DEAN OF ACTUARY. a British comedy of royal manmers by Courtney Wishbone.

Friendship without affirmation is like alienation without enmity.

The local government of village life was the genesis o f our Republican democracy. Vttiy ought we to exchange it for the corrupt amnesty of the tyrant or the faithless promises of our indifferent leaders. The unelected bureaucrats are now our shadow government.

There is a piety that tyrannizes and seeks conformity, leading, ultimately, to the censorship of conscience.

One cannot express chaos with chaos. The observer imparts a special order by way of his interpretation of events.

By its commutation of sentences of convicted felons, the California Supreme Court has attacked the idea of criminality while defending the behavior of the criminal. The jurists make it seem as if murder were a rhetorical mattter, since the full sentence of death is almost irrelevant.

The right of a court to subpoena information from the notes or files of a reporter is not an absolute right. There is a greater right — that of the people to know. E v e r y dictatorship commences with the control of Information.

A debt that falls due in its season is less to be feared than is a squandering out of season.

The pr e cedent of our heritage annoints the agency of human proposal of all our laws. Their stature derive s from the benign power of our Judeo-Christian ethic.

With every throw of his dice the gambler questions luck. Were he prescient. as he oft proclaims. he would win e-very time by abstention.

The value of a classical education is that it opens *w* p the possibilities of new interests, challenging innovation, critical appraisal and personal self-developmentJs Greek so far astray from politics? What about the Greek city-states? Is philosophy so distant from physics? What about Euclidian theory or the postulates of Galileo?

For a judge to subpoena newsworthy facts withheld by *sa* reporter is to make of him a discoverer of the facts, not an official who applies the law. He thus overreaches his authority. How can the judge have any substantive knowledge of the ramifications of the reporter's information when the trial is still in progress. How can he investigate "without prejudice." Indeed, is it his office t o investigate?

Time is a consequence of movement in space and imagination. It is that change and movement within the particular context of action which give to fiction its histori-can value as a social record of manners and morals, o f personalities and events.

The critic must be extremely wary of a colorful style, especially in criticism. It will lead you to say what you do not mean. It will seduce you into merely varied repetitions. It will trick you into making a climax instead of a basic statement." M. Bailey.

A faithful employee is better than a faithless wife.

The death penalty is the justice of righteous retribution.

If hate is the basis for security then the strength t o combat fear is missing, having produced instead of power spiritual impotence.

Under the Shield Laws why ought the judge to determine who m he will deny protection to if he is not privy to the information before it becomes trial evidence? To establish that all private news information falls within the judiciua tory powers of a judge, any judge, is to silence the criticism of an informed citizenry and, ultimately, lead to the propagandizing of information—today called "the pplltically correct" statement. The presupposition by the judge is that the information sought will aid the prosecution and u ph old, the law. The argument is specious.

The mantra of the coyote is for food, of man for solace.

A doctor a day keeps the pilli away. A pill a day gives the doctor his say. Neither is the prescription for health.

If the cow jumped over the moon, doth that not count for the presence of green cheeze.

"The old bird—he were a Calvinist truundtru—he said dey's much to gebottru luminations und understoffing."

"The unworthy man neds God's grace, it's true." "Do he—ven salvation's ist revocable?"

"Like an oath or a bill in the Congress, is it?" "Dot's vat I do be laming, sir."

—from THRUPENCE FROM THE CAPITOL, by Jettison Daggart, the blind playwright.

A democratic vote, when less than a majority in the turnout, promotes the abstention of opposition. It secures to itself the onerus of minority dissent, not the plea of majority acceptance.

Keep the door closed if you are afraid of wolves and the wind. For what other reasons did you build your house?

Taxes and the need thereof have long made out government con-fiscatory—from Shay's Rebellion to the formation of the IRS as an adjunct to Congress. At best, however, they are a civilized substitute for intercene warfare, a leveling influence, a sharing of the wealth.

The strength of the terrorist is his commitment. His world is one of alienation, its seeds those of discord, its drama the instantaneous mission, its hope that of momentary success and his will, at times, not even ideological. His world is also peopled by mummers and hierlings.

The terrorist lives within a psychological isolation there-fore he can form symbiotic, cooperative relationships with diverse ideologues who will, help his cause

The terrorist compartmentalizes easily and is swift to detect innocence of his presence and to exploit it the so f t underbelly of what used to be an unsuspecting world.

The Pleasure Principle operates in the ternorist's makeup. He takes almost exultant, sensual joy in the eradication of life that symbolizes opposition.

The terrorist is a sensualist, knowing no morals, no standard of decency, no sense of justice or equity, no wisd o m to discern good from evil. Those who do not belong to his camaderie are the evil ones.

Komenei is a religious fanatic and also a terrorist, willing to kill for the pleasure of his sensual desire for exultant power—which is Allah's will and purifies the devout. There is for him a catharsis, a perversity, a joy in killing.

Terrorism is therapeutic for its recruits, a remedy for the schizoid personality of alienation and camaderie.

The terrorist is an idealist corrupted by his own vain imaginings which, require force to succeed.

Power, to the terrorist, is the ascendancy of himself over those who are made go cringe before him. Its demonism demands the worship of the sons of hell.

We must fight terrorisn with firepower, commited to die for our freedom—or else remain out of sight, at home, silent, non-commited, mute and impotent. It is a dangerous world and always was so.

The attitudinized sylliogisms on an observed experience e prohibit the contemporary dramatist from escaping the char g e of subjective interpretation. The experiences depicted are rarely the experiences observed in reality, thus does his created fantasy become reality by adoption.

Terrorism has its acts of worship, its gods, its credo, its submission and "penetence," its zeal and applications to the world around. It is a quasi-religion,, sprung from the powers of darkness.

The anarchist is a terrorist within his own society. He eschews laws yet would take dominion over the enemy, the societally organized living under codes of law.

Keep the oath yet destroy the promise. Thus is the compact emptied of meaning.

A-moral reason never achieves true mercy by circumventing the justice of retribution.

Tell a woman you love her and she may doubt you, but tell her you have something to give her and she will trust you.

A will is the projection of the deceased. Ought not the stirring in the womb to perform the same office?

To be the Chairman of a powerful Congressional committee is to speak of people in the abstract. This distancing fosters alienation of government from the people.

Eat, drink and be merry—what was that last word? Gluttony is misery.

The "ends of power" are not power itself but that synergistic and unhindered capacity to manipulate laws and men. The power is inferred.

The sale of the farm was not nearly so painful as the loss of friends and neighbors. How great the calamity of t he latter, how transient the losses of the former.

All of the agencies and committees of government cannot put a Presidency back together again if he defaults ln his oath. Only a new regime can accomplish this.

Strong leadership in a government is neither demagoguer y nor oppression but the character and luminous minds o f representatives who put themselves third in the priority of public interests.

The Shield Laws that protect journalists and their sources of information imply, incontrovertibly, that the government will always be vulnerable to criticism by an informed citizenry. Their application admits of contructive evidence only and that's as it should be.

The judge in a Shield Law case is not empowered by fiat, constitutional mandate or adknowledged rules of evidence to decide to reveal the reporter's news source. To be so authorized—a liberal interpretation of judicial discretion under these trial circumstances—he must in effect discredit the witness and silence opposition, thereby relying upon his sole authority to give credence to the "missing" information. Is no other litigant in the trial to be trusted other than himself, the judge? There's a peculiar arrogance in this stance by a magistrate.

The spirit of free enquiry ought to animate a great university.

When they fail to vote, voters vacate their franchise. They abandon their suffrage, deeping it worthless. Choices have for them become oppressive, life-threatening, controversial and insignificant. Politically, they live in isolation from the rest of society.

A dead victim cannot forgive and so why does the court even deign to speak for him? It must then speak for the secondary victims of a crime, his loved ones.

The child, the infant and preadolescent citizen in America is pauperized by an insolvent government that knows no e n d to its deficit-spending. He is politicized, since the present onerous debt will eat up his future substance and condemn him to be an accomplice in the grand larceny of u n-controllable welfare. The child is therefore a negotiable entity.

Man's nature tends toward corruption, not eugenic perfection. The One-World envisioned by the eutopians exists only among the dead.

The politician who extrapolates his Christian humility t o embrace a world filled with evil is a fool. One does not prostrate one's nation to exemplify Gods piety.

Trial! lawyers reap a harvest of fees when they exploit the statutes of limitations.

Plea bargaining may diminish the docketl but it introduces the notion of extra-legal leniency.

Ghost profits enjoyed by lawyers from insurance claims a re a form of professional greed. They often support the industry's lobbyists.

A judge's sentence reduction harbors criminal intents

The heinous nature of the crime as against the leniency of the sentence is schismatic, dividing judge and jury, prosecutor and judge, plaintiff and judicial system,.

The liberal judgesr
- cannot bear to see a murderer die
- cannot enforce the death penalty
- fail to forsee the effect of their tolerance on society.
- find capital punish vengeful, not an acknowledgements of acccPuntability
- do not distinguish between justice and naked vengeance
- do not trust the jury system in the penalty phase
- do nor remember history, that criminal behavior r epeats itself
- are bllind to the side of the victim .'s survivors
- are amenable to the influence of liberal supporters in politics
- cannot distinguish between taking the profit out of crime and the profit out of the defense.
- see in their office the means to righting social wrongs

After the "big bang," what Agency produced order from the chaos?

If the evolutionists adhere to their closed system, as it is, to explain the universe, then they must admit of a faith in destiny, the destiny of continual improvement, Yet that faith implies direction and direction implies design. No design is fortuitous but must come from Mind, translated God. They cannot have it both ways.

The apparent loyalty of the terrorist to the cause? o f freedom is chimerical. His passion for freedom is his will to purge all (evil) opposition.

Terrorists are a coterie bonded by violence.

The terrorist seeks momentary power and attention., Intimidation is for him a weapon. His justice is vengeance.

The Anarchist is devoted to the law of the jungle. His loyalty is to <u>cause</u> rather than to <u>persons</u>.

The act of terrorism eliminates the sj&Mzoid feelings o f the terrorist "personality—who is a weakling. By the simple act of killing another human being—justified by his cause—he escapes the implications of schizoid and becomes a whole and harmonious person. He assumes a godlike dimension.

A play must invite the suspension of disbelief in the stage realities as life, while pre senting live human beings i n action. A movie challenges that disbelief with its r e-corded physical realism and by camera techniques—while presenting not a representation but an imitation of human beings in action. The imitation is two-dimensionalon the stage the representation is, of course, three-dimensional.

Appointees to high office in government belie the cane e pt of concensus or plebecite. Electors to high office canfirm the concept by popular choice. The former can greatly benefit the people by humane proposals, whilest t h e other can subvert the people by insidious petitions. Who is the man who can rightly judge another?

The soldier is honored for his participation in war, the terrorist is dishonore d for his failure to support his society. Duty animates one, flight the other.

There is a singular difference between the terrorists and the commited soldiers the one kills to justify self, his reason for existence while the other kills for an ideological reason within which he is thusexpendable and so neecfe no self-justification.

Do not accept the spur of another's guilt as if it were thjjne, for he seeks to lighten his burden on your account.

The thief is quickest to level the charge of thieverty. The congenital liar battens upon unsuspeatimg innocence.Think evil, speak and do innocence. Know the enemy.

A lie is best estopped with the txmth; another lie only compounds the slander.

Do not let a daughter of hell malign you with a manuf actured lie. Generally, the words themselves will bear t h e stanp of their source.

Mediocrity strives to level excellence out of envy.

Jealousy in a woman is the destroyer of the man. The face of innocence often masks the heart of evil.

Be wary of the jest that baits you to scoff ad the lusts of other men,.

Keep your spirits high with faith when scorned by evildoers.

The countenance of smiling friendship can hide the eye s for your weakness.

Better the solemn face that shows Idttle concern than the convivial mien of the foolish. For the one is a protection while the other exposes and makes vulnerable.

If you take another person at face value,, realize that it is only the face you assess.

Do not fulminate against the wiles of another lest you become bitter and rancorous.

The favored of good men is often the discarded of evil. Silence reproof and you save up for later rebuke. A mission postponed for to o long is rarely begun.

Do not let your anger metamorphose your innocence to appear unjustly wronged. The denial will only reinforce the malice.

Keep your conscience pure; do not dabble in wicked ways.

A false accusation wounds; an accusation proved to be true wounds even more deeply.

Hold fast to your morals. In tempestuous seas they a re your life raft.

You must have one gift. Find it. Cultivate it.

The self-righteous need no law for their support, since they support themselves and are righteous before their mirrored images.

Excellence in whatever endeavor is not to product o f but of diligent effort *over* time.

Cohabitation before marriage is the nemesis of commitment.

Know this, ye Christians, that satan does not have access to your thoughts unless you let him in.

The world maketh its followers weary through indulgence. It is the dissipation of constant self-gratification.

Bear no grudges toward a good man. His humanness ought to be respected.

Bo you listen to the whispers of sexual seduction? Rarely is the surrender spontaneous.

Relationship ? What is that but the mechanical interlocking of wants. Love is another matter entirely.

Steady, when under fire# There is no gain in retreat, perhaps only loss in advance. But living always requires movement in some direction.

Do not condemn yourself for frivolous reasons for such can be spiritual suicide.

Out of the abyss rises pain, chaos and misery. Many more would see were they not blind to God's alternatives.

It is not the number of men who follow a cause that d etermine its worth. It is the number of commited enlistees.

Quarrel if you must over picayune matters, but save your real friendship for the battles.

Do not fume over petty hurts; a good night's sleep will dispel most of them.

No one is perfect, especially yourself.

Temper triumph over another with empathy. Temper def eat at the hands of another with laughter.

A vision is rarely a vision if it is conceived in greed.

Trust your money to a beggar and he will beggar you r trust.

Do not be so fragile before the pummeling of another f o r his exercise can be your enlightenment.

Close up thy tent against the rain; thou hast a dry spot still on this earths A shrill voice bears little solace.

Subliminal suggestion may be beyond the control of the will but it is not beyond the shield of faith.

The trivial mind feels most at home in trivial matters. Itisi a waste of time to arouse it from its comfort.

A schoolchild can be brought to his book but cannot b e made to learn therefrom.

A rapacious person is less gratified by money as such than he is by ownership, for he seeks the power that possessions impart .

Keep nothing for the afterlife that you can distribute while you are living. Would you deny yourself the pleasure of your generosity?

Blame wrongly placed will return to curse your nights.

Rage is not an emotion that good men ought to cultivates It will in due course corrode the sensitive soul.

Sly jests contain subtle poison. Be wary.

Toilet humor—how ugly and repulsive, yet it is the mainstay in much of today's entertainment!

The image of material success and creature comfort—its chief seduction is social envy.

The false want of the advertising agency is the true bait of the sucker fish.

Would you glean praise like swept cobwebs from spiders nav gone? A Little humility will curb that appetite.

Try as hard as you will—you might just succeed,. Clever words bury ordinary thoughts.

Soar on the warm winds of the mountains and know that the verdant and liquid world Lies there below you.

Practice no vice, regret no corruption.

A man's perverse speech invites its own audience.

False accusations level fences.

A lying tongue invites revenge, a soothing tongue amity.

A false charge rarely seeks a balanced judgement.

A slanderous thought is the key to an open defamation.

Govern thy wicked opinion of another and so gain heaven's approval .

Slander will inevitably coldapse under the weight of truth.

The diminution of the character of another brings instant power and prolonged disgrace.

Would you ride to fame in the cortege of another's honor?

Keep thy slander for curses of the dogs; among them t h o u wilt be safe.

Take care lest a falsehood directed at another man miss its aim and strike a friend.

One can coin malice against another with little effort. I n deflecting it great painsmay not be spared.

Why should a man who is innocent of wrongdoing put up with slander when the justice of disproof lies close at hand?

A subtle insinuation is often more poisonous than an open accusation.

If you wish to bring a good man low, do not neglect to mention his failures in judgement.

Slander upon slander buildeth up a cache of corruption against the accuser.

The insults to a man's pride and honor will usually fall short of their mark if he but keep his distance.

Dishonor one good man and you injure all good men.

A false witness. what is he but a perjurer and a fraud?

A prodigal man counteth his wealth on the fingers of one hand.

Gossip is nothing more than slander resurrected.

A loose tongue and a capricious mind are the indellible marks of a fool.

A false witness makes of God a liar.

As one's boat glideth into Shool, so goeth the habitual slanderer.

To be prodigal is to belittle the value of thrift and, worse, to see not the ends of either,

The spendthrift is a prodigal—yet so, too, is the philanthropist. The one spends to gratify himself while the other invests to meed some need.

Prodigality does not always lead to poverty; compassion often controls the knife that divides.

If money could talk—it would oft keep silent, since it seeks not power of itself.

The subtle jest of the prodigal man is that he knows, ironically, his way will faille

Obedience—there is that which causes the cur to follow its master and that which governs discipleship between men.

A tyrant demands absolute obedience. A righteous man will yield before matters of equity and fairness.

Obey the law, as you must,, for in the obedience comes confidence in the actions of others.

As a child is taught to obey his parents—usually—so is a man taught to obey his government. Yet he must be careful not to confuse the two.

Every game in life *has* its rules the disobedience of which brings penalties.

Obey no man, law or force and you prepare for disaster. Obey little, want much.

To be prodigal is not always a bad action, since it may be the issue of a generous nature. Use discernment before condemning.

Obedience causes the lazy to suffer, whilest it often goads the ambitious.

Do not be slavish in your obedience of any man, for mortals err where fools fear to tread.

-8-

Synecdoche when used judiciously neither ornaments nor d extracts from a powerful style but, instead,, can summon other wood of experience to fuel the fire of passion.

A word's literal reference value is its semantic symbolism, its strict denotative utility, A word's non-literal reference value is of two sorts emotional, therefore connotatiw and designed to summon up emotional experiences associat e d with that literalness; and philosophical, as a doctrinal word within a system of thought, either secular or religious, or within a pattern of thinking peculiar to the author and logical to his argument.

To observe is not to arrest change, like a camera eye I n fiction the fluidity of phychological movement resides i n associations that accompany connotative descriptions of a characters actions, of an event unfolding, of a set ting for the story. Psychological movement is, indeed,, the quintessence of the stream-of-consciousness technique which attempts to be dynamic and mathematically literal at the same time. The literalness is denotative and an the surface, and the dynamics are in the subconscious connotations and associated referents that come to mind by the use of key surface words, clue words—the medium of suggestion by which the fictionalist with his lantern of synecdoche brings the past into present life.

Loyalty, if true and honest, must exclude and banish forever thoughts of treason and deeds of falsehood.

Loyalty is a virtue peculiar to Man alone; the liower animals bond through instinct .

Faithfulness is cousin to dependability, Loyalty has no peers.

Loyalty to one's country does not mean the slavish acceptance of all the government proclaims and does but, instead, is that voluntary willingness to support her founding principles in the written Law. Obedience to those laws ought to be tempered by their just enforcement.

Loyalty to a cause is temporal, to a state is conditional, and to a man is fixed and unshakeable.

Loyalty—most good men follow its prescriptions with little thought given to it. In times of crisis it become s a hungry tiger.

Dual loyalties, yes—but there is no such passion as a divided loyalty.

To be faithful is to be constant in one's attachments and actions. To be devious is its opposite and is filled with opportunism.

A man with great courage usually has great responsibility thrust upon him . Winston, Sir Winston Churchill was OTB of such men.

A man with courage may shrink back but go on; he who i s without the trait will lose many battles.

Courage becomes a man, just as beauty flowers the woman.

Physical courage—what is that but the capacity to endure physical pain. But morol courage, ah—there is w h e r e one's words and actions confront wickedness on the plain of desire.

We've heard often about the "work ethic." Why is w o r k "ethical" if not because in most circumstances of achievement work is the right <u>action</u>. The worker puts a value upon his sweat, upon his expenditure of time, upon works value to society and upon himself. To the lazy person, none of these values has validity.

Courage—one instills it in the young by encouraging them to reach beyond their imagined capacity. Successful in this the courage to take risks becomes habitual.

Thriftiness is not like a tool one picks up and lays down whenever chance dictates. It is a habit of mind, an attitude toward monetary performance that is ingrained. U se it wisely; it will support you in hard times.

Thrift is often the product of poverty times the years. I t is on occasion the result of avarice or penury. Rarely is it visionary, though it can be. Practice thrift if thou wouldst be secure.

The success of welfare derives from the thrift of productive citizens. The State only (mis)manages the money gotten there from.

We Americans have developed the Welfare State not bee a u se millions of people are needy but because those same millions have never learned how to manage their affairs properly.

Were the statistics known, chance would probably account for less than *1%* of those clamoring for State aid.

Our compassion has become a vice when we feel obligated t oɟ feed the world. Morally impelled, yes; responsible, no.

Compassion bears little resemblance to feeling. It is at best an attitude and an act.

Do not mistake stamina for persistence. The former is capacity, the latter is diligent application.

Many of the academic shortfalls in today's schools could be solved by a strict enforcement of one word: <u>application</u>.

Fine teaching falls on deaf ears. Great teaching cannot a-rouse the dead to knowledge.

Persistence—what is it but the use of the age-old rule o f seeing things to their completion?

Welfare beggars honest labor.

Know this, that for every welfare recipient there must be at least three administrators: one to collect the money, one to issue it and the third to manage the recipient.

Genuine poverty must be addressed, genuine sloth, never. Cheat on your tests, schoolboy, if you would cheat in life.

Cheating is no more than an admission of inadequacy. produced by disinterest ., laziness. procrastination, distracttions, more important matters. fatigue and a general at titude of indifference. Modern-day schoolchildren are afflicted by all of these and yet—dismayed parents blame conscientious teachers. Poor parenting cripples learning.

Trespass if you will. Ask for forgiveness as you must. Vandalism is the excrudescence of wickedness and ignorance.

Vandalism of an ideological nature is satanic. If the latter is an acceptable cult then so, too. is its ugly offspring an acknowledged credo.

What jury is fair that admits of bias? And yet where in all mankind is there a man who is totally neutral?

Property symbolizes one's labor—and one's failures and successes.

From wealth grows property and from property grows wealth. They are inseparable.

Join the Vandals, destroy a church—as they once did through out parts of Europe.

The wealth of a nation is not measured by its treasury but by the investments of its citizens in enterprises of merit. Through hobbling laws we have largely curbed the latter, therefore our wealth has diminished.

Mediocre men seek power over men of excellence and stature.

The mob justifies its presence with violence and its "mind" with random acts of destruction.

No two participants in a mob scene would think alike d id they not carry placards. Therefore. the consensus of a mob is a fiction—and a very dangerous one. For the fiction, if carried far enough, leads to annihilation.

Seize a man's property and you put him in irons.

The liberal media are not generous, as the word infers, but they are dedicated to a closed system of ururpation. They would have all greatness, advances and benefits of a society attributed to their efforts.

The chief purpose of modern-days drug abuse is to promote in the user a euphoria, with or without the inspiration of pain. Boredom| peer-pressure and smartness are other causes.

What is there to forge t—since we live in times of affluence, unless it is the guilt of a bad conscience? How great is the cost of mindless escape!

Do drugs, do death.

A man who steals from a friend steals from his own character.

Take a lesson from the panther when it climhs to the topmost limb of the tree. It does not cheat on its quarry but b y its very nature assumes a superior perspective of advantage.

Not all pastors are annointed. Their private lives de m on strate this.

If you must hoard, keep what is useful and relevant rather than enjoyable.

Censorship is the curse of free expression, for not only does it oppress but it denegrates and destroys. Indeed, the Censor will always knock at the gate of freedom to gain entry into the heart and mind of the gatekeeper.

Property—it doth oversee all other possessions of merit but love.

The weapon is a prehistoric invention., Does it not suggest mankind's natural wickedness? And his failure to progress?

Replay the bloody cries of the mob if you would hear the oblations to terror.

Vandalism, it is a curse upon a civilized community of men.

A trade skill is not. a novel invention of the Medieval Guilds but a sustaining way of life for the traveler and shopkeep.

Why would you hoard if you were not fearful of shortages unless you build your stores to proclaim your triumphs2

A censorious person is not necessarily a pious person.

Save what you have little use for if you would deal in rummage.

The sacrifices of war lie on the altar of Victory. Any outcome short of victory is a waste of lives.

The compromises in wartime are frequently the advantages in peacetime.

Forgiveness borrows most often from compassion and rarely from retribution.

If thou wouldst be forgiving, be also comforting.

Folk medicine was the pragmatic application of limited reagents to impossible conditions. Sometimes the remedy worked, sometimes it did not. The placebo effect was not uneard of even way back then.

If clothes maketh the man, why extol the man within t he clothes?

One goes to great pains to clothe beauty yet sometimes succeeds merely in hiding it.

If "appearances are everything," why try? Just put on the dog and be done with matters.

Repentance belongs to no one, since it is the soul yearning to see God.

Romance used to mystify the naive. Now it angers the jaded.

Most people nowadays want privacy both ways—personal and public. But that is an impossible state in a mobile society.

The government's invasion of the citizen's privacy spells the end of old institutions—marriage, parenting a n d family, schooling and property ownership. It also augers a propagandistic control of the press.

From its corporate body the church will cast *out* the hidden infidel yet show another face to the world that invites sinners to come in.

Christ's church is a congregation of believers — that a-lone. Then why must it purge those who fall short o f man's standards?.

Cleanliness is not "next to Godliness" so much as it its next to good hygiene.

Politicians promote their image which. fixed in the mind, resists change by circumstances. An intense disillusion men t develops there from in the body politico The lack of sound ideological: statements only compounds the alienation.

Grow a face. assume an office.

Splatter the opposition with shit if thou wouldst be artful .convincing and successful in politics. Fingerpaint therewith on the windows of the naive.

"Are you going to the poll to vote?" one neighbor asked another. "No," the second replied. "I'm going to check out my friend's house." Quaint exchange!

A social class was never such until a sociologist invented the wage scale, borrowing heavily, of course, from Brit i s h notions. Neither education nor possessions define them i n America but investments delineate the differences.

Keep repentance to yourself if you distrust the offended. Ah attitude of forgiveness belies the intention to injure. Outcasts are the symbols of a pietistic purge.

Welcome solitude as an old friend; it comes without begginfe or demanding. It comforts, restores and recaptures Host time.

Do not sacrifice to an unknown person or cause for that way is suicide.

What was not wanted is no sacrifice.

The Government does not generate taxes but only manipulates them.

Taxes are les and les representative of the people, not because of their inequities, but because of their manner of seizure. The IRS will! always excuse its deformed will by pointing a finger at the Congress.

<u>Historical Revisionism</u> is an insidious device to shape our past as a nation to fit the selfish demands of the present.

Hospitality to a stranger on the road was once a shibboleth.

It has become a curse, for who will give lodgings to a murderer?

Revise American history then, you rogues of academia, if you would dimish our stature in an envious world.

Gangs are the blackguards in an insolvent community. Their survival depends more upon tolerance than it does fear o f them.

The immigrant to America is not a novelty, just his desire to preserve his island untouched by natives.

Image is in politics what it is in religion—an icon to be admired if not worshipped.

Gangs are often a curse to their own families, and yet they have mainly themselves and not community to blame. Gang s are the products of morally empty households.

Pornography and pedQphilia are the spawn of satanic darkness. Accursed and poisonous, they thrive on patronage.

The license of sexual perversions is the gateway to moral turptide in the schools. Once swing back the bars and protection of the children is gone.

The clandestine smile is the covert insult.

Violence truckles to hate. From where else cometh its energy?

The alien may be a native who is more foreign in his o w n country than the immigrant. Be perceptive of such as they.

If thou wouldst destroy the family, then only the government remains to raise the new generations.

The traditional family stands athwart the tide of bastardy. Destroy it and legitimize irresponsible conduct.

A life style may be fad or fashion. It takes little initiative to start one.

Independence was invented when slavery was inaugerated. B e-fore that there was freedom.

Social classes are a figment of the Idealogue. For him tradition is an unfavorable force which he has yet to understand.

Prayer in public schools is not foreign to America. Only the lie of a rogue in Congress would make it so.

Clothes speak for a culture. The closer to the culture, the farther away the wearer thereof. A suit of armor and a velvet gown both say something about their respective cultures.

The chief crusade of a street gang is revenge against another gang. Their barbarity is obvious. Their members represent one of the lowest forms of civilized life in our cities.

Violence becomes a thing treasured when it is the only means of expression. Some murderers take erotic pleasure in homicide. others embrace death like an on-going and repeated form of suicide. Still others respond to the call of the demons. Dementia is a constant.

Do not scoff at independence lest it slip away from thee unawares.

Situational ethics is a plea for indecision and a reliance upon feelings as motive.

The outcasts of any societies were once the the in-bred of earlier societies—the gladiator, the prostitute, the daredevil.

The prototype of the outcast was the female baby of ancient times.

Look into the heavens and see movement without migration. Does that not speak of design?

In the early West there were gangs on horseback, terrotories to be defended, objectives for pillage, rape and robbery. Do not be dismayed that the gang-spirit lives on.

Appearances do not always deceive. Consider the snarl of the beast.

Arm yourself with the weapon of language if thou wouldst combat a lawyer.

The rabble-rousers, did they not exist in the days of Jesus Christ and Paul, the Apostle? Indeed, street gangs endangered the lives of each.

If thou wouldst "break the close," have thy excuse ready.

The sacrifice with blood fulfilled an ancient covenant. Is not war much the same?

Prosperity leads a man astray when its promises fall short of fulfillment.

The compulsion to hoard is territorialism, symbolized.

Property represents the wealth from a man's labor, the wealt h of another transferred into his hands, and still a third the wealth of the State held by permission.

Romance attracts until the passion runs out. Then it must be regenerated by acts of commitment.

In our times persistence is derided as a disease for which the cure is perpetual vacation and frivolity.

Slander God with blasphemy, appease satan with calumny.

Censorship ought never to go beyond the dictates of suggestion and example. There is much to be said for the latter.

Wouldst thou steal thy neighbor^ horse? Then let him steal thy barn in equity.

Censorship is to some extent a warrantee for the survival of honored values. Which takes precedence makes all the difference in the world.

A man who repents without pride is a student of the Sage. Curry favor with power, reap the corruption thereof.

"To get even" implies a recoverable loss that is best addressed by vengeance. Retribution implies a recoverable gain extracted from justice.

Save a little, squander much is the code of the prodigal.

A willingness to lead is often attached to a reluctance t o lose.

A good wife is an impediment to a lazy husband.

It is a sinister occupation to make public sport of a private life for it sets a craven precedent.

There is strength in a humility that is gained through self-discipline. The cringer, cm the other hand. is humbled by his fear.

An insecure man is often arrogant or swaggering. An insecure woman is frequently shrill or mute.

"Conventional wisdom" and common sense are one. Thomas Paine knew this.

Among most gold was less a fever than a passion of greed in 1849. Their farms. their jobs, their savings were not enough.

Scout the rapid before you shoot it, for there's no time t o change course in the boil.

The charm of the wilderness is a dream that will leave its visitors unprepared for nature.

You got a beef on the job? Tell it to the cockata. and let him decide o.

Old buildings and older spirits still, inhabit the West o f today.

Permissivle trespass is the privilege of a friend, impermissible trespass is the offense of an enemy.

-9-

Ours is the age of information, yet it is obviously dissociated from wisdom. The decline of the family, of public morals; corruption in government, a disease of epidemic proportions, and great unhappiness testity to this calamitous lack. Only a return to our Judeo-Christian heritage can save this nation from directionless mediocrity.

In some circles a man is disreputable if he uses his hands for work.

Literature is the voice of the past speakimg to the present.

Literature bestows no honors except the acknowledgement o f its honesty.

When the perverse shoves good taste aside, corruption takes over an art form.

The critical evaluation of a work of fiction must begin with certain important relationships between the structure of reality and the structure of language. Doubt as to the meaning of a passage, a character's actions, his motives, the author's commentary, the skepticism that intervenes between content and recognizable parallels by the reader can so dominate his interest (in jargon calles the "motor-effective attitude") that the value of the content as sense experience, as ideology, as human insight, as intelligent understanding, can be effectively hampered. Communication is thereupon altered. Ambiguity and reader confusion that result diminish the effectiveness of the author's poorly communicate d meanings. If the reader is uncritical and undiscriminating his attitude will often become negative.

The literary value, aesthetic or dramstic, and pragmatic sense perceptions are thereby hard to weigh in the light of personal experience. This is so by reason of the fact that the reader is not aware that the ambiguity exists at all, or knowing that it does finds it hard to assign values to experiences "recreated by words." Fantasy and reality merge.

Entertsinment is also a part of the content value of the recreated experiences in fiction, drama, poetry. Enjoyment derived from any one of these forms by the audience is a n essential part of his participation. He internalizes what he sees or reads, sharing with the author the experiences of ideological conflict, physhological combat, intellectual interplay and the entire range of sensuous presentation. T o the extent that he is not entertained, deriving pieasure therefrom, he has not shared the author's inner life.

For a long time it has puzzled me that the democrats, w ho admire and extol the "laboring man," inevitably elect a man of wealth to office to represent them,, Perhaps he is their surrogate father.

Why ought privacy to be an issue for debate when it never was so to America's founders? Indeed, it was settled in Jun e of 1790 that "the people had a right to be secure in their persons, houses, papers, and effects,, against unreasonable searches and seizures." (Art. IV) Patently, Madison a n d others had established what they thought was anincontes table law.

A false witness is a failed juror in the court.

Slander is sometimes believed in by its very own speaker.

License gives rise to prodigality. Each is irresponsible. Simply put, obedience is conformity under pressure to do so. Courage is the arbiter of a task without precedent.

A clever fool is more highly esteemed than as stupid servant.

The vision of a spendthrift is his hindsight.

The members of the United States Congress enjoy the privileges of Class. There's no other way to describe the emoluments they enjoy.

Perpetuated in office by an indifferent public, our Congressmen thrive on the status quo.

A Republican bows to precedent, a Democrat to the shadow of the past.

A lie from the lips of a liberal Democrat is a message from God in a Democratic Congress, from a Conservative Republi can it is a memo from hell.

Congressmen are adroit at bonding themselves to their office with bribes known as Porkbarrel grants.

Property is a stigma to the radical zealot. Give him a dou$i nut and he'll feed his dog.

Would you trust the keeper of a lion's cage? How rauch safer it is to trust the Chairman of a Congressional committee.

The savings of the "little man" rarely become the inheritance of his children when the Democrats conquer Congress.

A liberal Democrat is like a horse that is blind one eye. His vision of the future is defective, and he depends upon the headless rider of a Republican president for his spurring.

Chiefly lawyers make it to Congress because they are adept at twisting words and arms.

Globalism is t he shibboleth of international equalityas if to be superior were immoral and reprehensible.

Denounce a new law if you would see it bounce into permanence.

Sexual perversion is a choice. So, too, is riding motorcycles.

Vandalism is so despicable that it defies all categories.

To the savage caveman the club was his weapon; it is of ten the same for contemporary man.

Why would anyone want to rouse the rabble unless it was in pursuit of an unpopular cause?

The deviant pastor is a solace to the demons.

Not since <u>God.s Little Acre</u> has the public so enjoyed a preacher's clandestine ways as they have before the T V evangelists. Sensationalism has taken on a spiritual meaning.

Religious fraud primarily rubukes God for his leniency.

The solitude of the mountaintop is anathema to the dweller in the city.

Sell the farm, they covet your land. Buy a farm, they envy your produce. The world wants it both ways.

Kindness to animals is a virtue, for why should a man put out the light of life for the fun of it?

Pornography mirrors misogyny.

Blame others for your own mistakes and you'll never improve your performance.

If you'd survive in the winter, prepare in the summer. How fundamental to life itself!

It is better to barter a square foot of land than it is to sell an acre at a loss.

Land is rarely infertile to some crop. Rather, the farmer is too lazy to try.

The historical revisionists would standardize lies.

Religious convictions lead more men astray from God than unvoiced doubts in the faith.

A religious faith without convictions is an empty premise.

Regard the devout. how often they look behind to assess their following, how seldom ahead to judge their way.

Corruption in the church is no less frequent than is corruption in the government. It is simply ritualized t o make it acceptable.

The church and state are severable on these ground that the former can never supply the deficiencies for the latter, that the priest or pastor can never administer the secular law.

Good men will eagerly destroy what generations before them have erected, the monuments to achievement. The iconoclasts are the spoilers.

The blessings of the faithful are often the pleasures o f the infidels.

The church is chartered of God, the prison of hell, yet one cannot exist without the other.

To make restitution is ancient Hebraic law; it was also the justice of the Mamrourabi Code (theft of the proper t y of church or state-that seignior shallx be put to death,") and of the Roman Tribunal. Why then ought criminals to be set free in these days?

Change the situation, adjust the ethics of conduct and *eyih* men will prove honest. The reasoning is specious.

A faith that accommodates all perspectives saves none.

The secular state will devour the religious community if they forsake their beliefs.

Be forewarned that a pious man who wishes to make the most of his religion will proclaim his stature from the housetop.

Unprincipled men find religion a suitable toy for investment. capricious men find it a pasttime, and diligent men an enterprise to exploit.

The harbinger of alienation is the promise to God unfulfilled.

Would you do damage to your neighbor? Then hope that some way you can manage his affairs.

Understand the subtleties of the matter that when a man of fers to help you he may be ingratiating himself into you r concerns.

Weigh the words of one who is quick to promise. They may be found wanting *im* the scales of integrity.

Do not regard with envy another man's wealth. After all it is not yours, and the exercise is a waste of your time.

True courage is not the mask of pretense but the soul of true risk.

Denegrate a friend and you shake his trust; charge an enemy and you quicken his defense.

Cooperative effort will bring results. Creative chaos will bring dismay.

Do you live where the mountains grow wild in the fury of the storm? Be grateful that meddling man has no control over the scene.

While shooting the rapids of the Colorado I heard the canyon wren compete with the roar and was amazed.

Violence rarely comes alone but rather runs with a gang o f events.

There.s nothing like the rape of our nation by illegal immigrants to demonstrate our vigor! But who wants it?

Better to live in isolation and endure alone than to thrive amidst the throng and batten on plenty.

Rest assured that to the extent that we surrender our enfranchisement through apathy, the enemies and aliens of our nation will gain the hill.

All we need do to destroy America is do do nothing.

For over forty years we have looked up to the rest of the world and now we find ourselves short in pride and statiure.

On a lonely country road every passerby is a stranger. I n the city teeming with manswarms the same is true. Why ought one to chose the crush of the latter instead of the freedom of the former?

Careful habits curry efficiency.

Be cautious at the crossroads, for someone may have altered the signposts.

Games of chance are the mark of an indolent age; they a bound at every corner in today's society.

The credo of the robber is—take no chances; of the entrepreneur it is—take the risks.

Waffle on your promises and syrup with your excuses.

Autonomous of God, the judges in this nation can declare the <u>family</u> to be whatever their wicked hearts dictatesa boy and a man, two men, two women, a woman and a dog, a man and his daughter. Society tolerates this corruption of the abyss because they know not God, being gods themselves.

Save a penny, save a dollar. The one frequently leads to the other.

Do not rely upon the censor to discern the poison in a work of art but, instead, perceive if the piece was intended to give offense. If so, wouldst thou stand idly by and drink thy dram of hemlock?

I'm sure there are some aspects of hell that are highly creative. But wouldst thou be downturned instead of u p-lifted for the sake of novelty?

The powers of darkness are stronger than the imagination. Given a crack, they will filter into the sanctuary of your mind.

Mind control—thine own or hell's. The choice is yours.

If thou be curious about the regions of hell, pray Go d to lead the tour. For if thou, travel alone the entrapments and the mysteries and the seductions of fiends may damn thee forever. Do not play on the edge of fate.

False repentance is a consolation to the hypocrite.

Social classes, what are they but sad groupings by the Shamans of sociology?

That leader is rapacious who would strip the product of a man's sweat from him and give it to the indolent.

In the Congress there are blackguards who believe that the American taxpayers exist for their pleasure. They bribe their way into office with the money of others, and they claim "perks" to enhance their prestige.

Statesmanship is the quality of listening to the will of the people and of responding to their needs—inconeert with the rest of the nation.

The children are doing poorly in school because their parents are doing poorly at parenting.

How can you inspire your child to read when you neither read nor shelve any books in your house?

How can a class of adolescents appreciate <u>Treasure Island </u>when they listen to the tweeky, little voice of a woman teacher read the dialogue of Long John Silver or Cap tain Smollett?

He who idles away his time knows not the hour.

The fascination of television is lethal to creativity.

Play with chance, garb opportunity.

Immigration is the soul of the wanderlust.

Violence, repeated, betrays the destructive side of man's natures

The destruction in violence is anathema to the burgeoning in creation. Is the former so oppressive it must be done?

The political image is the social reflection as the adultery of one is the adultery in the other. It's a sad commentary on these times that society is obsessed by what is between the legs rather than what's on the shoulders.

Sacrifice—soldiers and the loved ones of the slain know what it is. All else is commentary.

A liberal press disdains the Christian because he is an easy target and keeps no lobbyist in Washington.

What has always piqued my curiosity is the cavalier attitude of many Congressmen toward their duties. They ought, to b e removed from office.

Much is made of property in Ameica. In the rest of the world the common people own no property. It's symbolic of the citizen's power and independence.

Environmentalist!!, when militant . can lead only to the rap e of property ownership and its seizure "for the public good." By declarations of <u>public domain</u> the government will! aceomplish its evil purpose.

Take the land away from the people and you make them politically impotent. Take away their savings and you destroy them. Take away the power in their votes and you demolish their birthright. Take away their natural rights and you damn the nation to mediocrity and decline. Having cost the people these treasures, you in power will never again inspire them to recapture our glorious past. You will ha v e leveled America to the status of a peasant nation where abject obedience and the mediocre attemptrare ways of life.

The feminist movement is largely economic requiring politics to effect its ends. And yet were all their wishes to be granted at once they, the feminists, would still yearn for male power.

The feminists. clamor for male power is not to share but to control.

True repentance is not in the least akin to apology,, Clever at cards, dull with money.

A gambler free began his spree, and he ganbled away until a quarter to three when—his luck broke.

Censor a lie, then doubt the truth.

The sting of death is not the fear of it but the terror o f it.

Persistence hath many friends but only one enemy—laziness.

Save a penny today, a penny tomorrow—it is the habit that counts most.

Be loyal to those deserving of it. for loyalty to a fool is nonsense.

Slander against a good man is like a jug of bilge water thrown into the wind.

How the liberal press protects its own and exposes the favorites of others.

The small confidence gotten from understanding is worth a thousand assurances born of misunderstanding.

Carefully pare away the skin of a hard situation and you will find an elemental conflict of choices at the heart.

The prelude to a fratracidal war is alive in the seeds of early dislike. Therefore foster companionship i f you would reduce later sibling rivalry.

First merit the praise if you would sustain the acclaim.

Turn not away from a hard task lest it meet you at the next turn.

If you would stand in the way of another's obsession be prepared to do battle.

Do not mark the simple desires of the childish heart, for they may some day reappear as a grand design for t h at life.

The most forward of sinners can be the most backward of penitents. Show compassion as did the Lord.

For some men leadership is a must. for others it is a choice and still for most it is an improbability.

Does the mother who hastens her brood in out of t he rain think of herself? Nay. and so it ought to be with those who lead a trusting people.

Make a bosom friend of mercy. She will avail thee much in the face of human suffering.

Do not fancy that thou understandest grief before thou has lost a loved one. There are some treasures you will never redeem except by tears and then, only dimly.

"Clear the way!" shouted the old farmer driving his horses recklessly along the dirt road. "I've slops for the pigs and I go to market."

"Let me see your nicest pirouette," said the dancing master.

"I haven't learned the pirouette, sir." "Then—let's have, say, a hop or two."

"I haven't learned how to hope, either, sir—since I am not a rabbit."

"What about a run and a—a leap, like the fox over t he hedge?"

"My only foxes are at the zoo, sir."

"Well then, what can you do—since you've hired me to tea c h you how to dance?"

"Dance! I thought you were going to show me how to fly."

—from Act I, Sc. ii, of "The Flying Ballet Instructor," by Jo M. Smudge, of the Royal Court.

The more voluminous and windy your speech, peppered with quotes ad infinitem and pro bona, nolo contender e, the less one learns therefrom.

"You're in classic good health and your hold your shape admirably," the doctor said to his patient. "I don't und e r-stand."

"That's because X practice with me shadows," said the slender woman in gentle tones, smiling her shadowy smile.

—from the magazine "Agglutination," in an article by Dr. E. Forcepts.

The admirable mismatch is the most ideal couple of today. In ail things they get along well in their mutual absence.

Do not throw rocks at the house of a neighbor, since his house is an extension of himself and deserves respeet.

The petty gesture is usually the expression of a quarrlesome nature.

One can best follow the trail of a leader by seeing his vision before imitating his steps.

Have you never climbed a mountain before? Always prepare for the descent.

The way of the lizard is forthright and dusty, the flight of the swallow is devious yet fixed, the way of the lion is secret and hungry. From these learn how you ought to confront evil.

Human mistakes are many. Why do you trouble to remember them all.

The alien in a new land will who is shown too much generosity will exploit it for his own gain.

Cultivate the wise if you would share new insights.

When the lightning strikes on the nearby rocks, draw u p thy knees and sit upon the coil of thy hopes. They are the insulation far the future.

Do not try the patience of a trusting man or else he will look for thy counterfeit plea.

Grief is a passing condition though the sorrow may linger on. Have no remorse about these things, for they are a part of life as well as of death.

Hold fast to those who know your heart. They will stay you in the storm.

Small minds are most often given to petty deeds of reprisal. Every parent has an emissary away from home.

If you would trifle with the reputation of an honest man, then be ready to defend thy smugness.

Anger without cause can be ruinous. Anger with cause can be a corrective.

This nation has long stood on the premise that every individual possesses an intrinsic value. Yet if God is dead i n the schoolroom then only the System awards value. The intrinsic, the inalienable, value is gone and we are awash with the proud swill of human propositions. Think on that.

WARNING ON THIS LABEL: the iconoclastic documentary of today will be accepted tomorrow as the true history of our past. In the image lies the power to generate belief.

Conformity is the refuge of mediocrity.

A loan that is met with an easy promise ends up in bankrupcy.

Give to your friends, lend to your enemies for against them you still have recourse.

You are on trial all your life for your misdeeds. You seldom take the stand for your charity.

Do not trivialize your good works by false humility lest another who is less gifted preempt your due praise.

Show good courage where courage needs to be shown. 0 n other occasions the world may accuse you of arrogance.

Kindness is not weakness. It is the reluctance of a strong man to deal a harmful blow. Staying his hand he confronts the charge of cowardice. Dealing the balm he awaits the cry of effete. Suffering the weaker to survive he stands to be accused of dereliction in his duty. Finally, enduring these calumnies, he confesses his limitations.

Accept a compliment with grace. If it was sincere, your return responded in kind. If insincere, then hypocr is y required no other answer .

Learn to judge between false praise and genuine praise. The former begs a rival answer, the latter affirms a true premise.

When in doubt about the motive of another person, al ways hold your judgement in abeyance lest you be proved wrong and seem perverse.

There is no discredit to trying a new path with small incursions. The method simply lacks boldness of execution.

All art invites comment. Great art inspires admiration. Petty art denegrates its audience while fine art gives rise to imitation. Under each of these parabolas, the audience reflects back the character, nature and quality of the art. As the audience changes, so, too, does the reflection.

Would you fly a kite without a wind? Then why raise the cry "Enough!" without a sound issue to present. Protest without substance can never take wing.

Scriptures say much about sin, mankind's wrongdoing against a righteous God. Yet if he pleads innocence he must plead non-involvement with life, where wrongdoing is rife, call it sin or not. Do not beg the issue of crime by ruling out God.

Our enjoyment of life is proportionate to our involvement with others. It is disproportionate to our flight from reality. It coexists with our natural affinities. I t shrinks before our apathies.

Bear no memory of a wrong that was unintentional, for then you ascribe to innocence the character of malice.

Literature that appeals to prurient interests is not literature, regardless of the fine style and the presence of literary devices. Its characters and story define the elements of a poison so potent that it rules out all perceptions of events but the lewd. Simply put, poisonous literature specializes in poison that drugs the mind and the emotions. The notion of a "redeeming social purpose" is a nonsensical shibboleth that merely potentiates the poison.

If you would salvage a lost opportunity, you must first borrow from that experience to modify the ambition. I n common parlance, that means "tradeoffs."

Do not ply a total stranger for sympathy in goals lion g sought after yet never realized. What has he to do with your quest? Keep your own counsel.

If you would take your neighbor into court for some fancied grievance, be certain that a dishonest lawyer will plead your case.

Sports for money was once the small reward that player s sought in recompense for their time and skill. Million dollar appetites for money now rule the old games. The sport has become the recompense for the money.

Unmotivated students will destroy classroom learning when given the opportunity. At that point, bootcamp discipline ought to commence {t'ruly, I have found it quite effective.

Allow a child through his growing years to continually have his way and he will treat society with the same disdain and presumption. He must still get his own way but will encounter resistence.

It is rubbish to assert that poverty is the cause of crime. The failure of the parents to indoctrinate their children with the concordant values of ethical right and wrong is the major cause.

Discipline denied is discipline accepted by youth uncared for. That is an anomaly.

Purient literature is propaganda for lust.

What is lascivious in a literary work is largely denotative. How can it then be misconstrued unless on purpose?

The proof of fine writing is not on the degree of arousal it elicits but on the magnitude of its perceptions a bout life.

"Good taste" is the hackneyed phrase of another age, for what offended then most certainly does not now. "Proportion" is a word more germane to our day and society.

"The intention of the writer" was once a theme for sc hool children to write about. Why have we cast that jewel aside?

A court that promotes the lewd by feigning its protect ion injects into society the lewdness of its magistrate(s).

"Community standards" is a test long held valid. The purveyors of smut would exploit the community for its mo n e y while overriding its values for their profits. Can they legally have it both ways?

Lascivious judges are the supporters of pornography, in the name of "freedom of expression." They draw those lines that will not hamper their office. They compel the majority to tolerate what disgusts it. The freedom of the lewd is t o them the bellwether of progress. They make of freedom a plain without boundaries. They eschew censorship by the court in lieu of their tyranny to mandate obscenity and call it "the law." Liberal judges are the accomplices in crimes against all reasonable standards of decency. Why ought they to be allowed to make literary judgements?

Corrupt the children and you condemn the future.

The abuse of a wife is the despicable act of a non-man. Jail is too good for him.

Trifle with gender and you trouble the mature.

The innocence of a child is like "the pearl of great price." Once lost, it can never be recovered.

Age with grace means, modest Limits on youth. Do not hasten the process. Do not let others rush you.

Society thrills to find an object for its misplaced compassion. The homeless is one such, for they are not abandoned waits of the street. They are privileged migrants into the world of irresponsibility.

Control your imagination so as to avoid the slew and you'll rarely be troubled by a bad conscience.

A dog that barks often may share his owner's obsession with trespass.

Capture the tiger by its tail and you prepare for its meal.

The prototypical housewife never stayed at home. That is a myth. She stayed in the tents of other men. That is the reality.

If you would work for justice, first sheer the sheep o f their self-righteous warmth. Make the contenders go bare.

A remembered mistake oft troubles the sleep of the conscientious. Only its correction promotes rest.

A child at play was once admirable; now the conduct is reprehensible to many—since it costs money.

Why ought every new tax to be imposed without the consensus of the people? It is extra-legal for the Congress to do so yet porkbarrel projects mollify the constituents and gag those taxed.

The blind man finds his way with a stick; this method is not unlike that of the Congressman who finds his way with a stick—either "big" or packaged with a carrot.

The sting of spurs sets the horse off at a gallop. The sting of a Presidential rebuke sets the Senate into a dither.

Pair off a Republican against a Democrat on the floor and you have a fight, in the Congressional coffee room, a choice of condiments, in the Committee Room, a brawl and old-lawyer arrangements, and in the community — identical twins.

Throw no ropes, die down no projects.

Interpretive differences are the bane of evangelists and lawyers. Have they not heard that the truth is never *m* guess?

A poem is an emotional experience. The poet is required to give voice only to his own true perceptions. Though he may read aloud, he speaks to one listener at a time. A poem is an intimate confidence, a peculiar perception, a valued surmise.

Much counselling tends to mechanize human relationships.

Do not squander the text of your most intimate raptures for the pleasure of an indifferent audience.

Would you embrace the problems of another in order to purge your own? Perish the thought! Shariing is never purgation but mutual enlightenment.

Lean not too hard on the shaky proposition of "I love you." It does not always bear up well under dead weight.

The novelist is the tale bearer for his generation .He writes not to be seen but that *hks* books be remembered. Hs writes because he must, and that is an intimate matter. He writes to know who he is in time and where he stands in space o n this planet. He writes to discover what he truly believes, feels and thinks. He writes to separate himself from anonymity, for his great fear is not failure in his writing but failure to discover who he really is while he is alive. He is the most individual of all men, working in the laboratory of humankind, paid chiefly by satisfaction in his craft and endowed with an unconquerable spirit for survival. What his work gives his and future generations is of inestimable value as a window into another time and place. If h e is an honest writer his revelations will be honest—a n d personal, never counterfeit and indifferent.

Take no thought of the distortions of malice. Your achievement is the measure of your integrity, your performance the scaleweight of your will, and your stature the confidence of a more kindly world.

Do you beat upon your plowshare to make a sword? Sir, you must first heat up the forge of a passionate crusade t o white hot.

Warm your desires over the coals of defeat and they will puff into flame with your tending.

To butcher the noise you must first slaughter the pig.

The raging waters of the storm will quickly change the pastoral bent.

Carry your own weight if you'd take full pleasure in your mutual enterprise.

A song lost is never fully recaptured, only its similitudinous notes.

I've yet to see a musician who thought his instrument was in tune before the music began.

Five handsful of salt will no longer buy a horse—but may bring a cow to water.

Throw away your skill if you think you must but thus emptied, do not charge God with fraud.

Follow the scent that popularity leaves if you have a liking for dung. Just as no committee can create great art, no populace can write great literature.

The likes and dislikes of the public are fickle., Consider how the ratings change each year, and the rat of production runs around in its little wheel cage.

Better to die unknown and unloved than to have lived as aivillain.

Keep your task in the focus of your mind if you would succeed at a thing.

Delineate your objectives, compound your accomplishments. Frail thoughts bring feeble resultse

A constant and daily attention to your soul will bring you great strength. From the Holy Scriptures we can learn much about worthy men.

Do not ever regard the world with smug piety. It is yours to live in whether or not you like it, and it will not change to suit your desires. Enjoy it, relish the company of others whom you deem inferior, though in God seyes this may not be so. Cultivate a love for those who suffer; accept your own hardness of heart as a verity of your own life. Do not give i. to petty misdeeds. Champ ion the winners but applaud the losers. Life is a battle one way or the other, and none of us knows the future with any certainty. Live, enjoy, create. Thou hast worth.

Power breeds power. Never forget that. Merely be apprised that it is so and, finding the source, look about you for its rays.

Let a hobby occupy your troubled thoughts. You can do no worse.

Wishful thinking is the pasttime of the foolish, for i t is a waste of time, as we all know, yet it can lead to unhappy delusions.

We sit upon the mountain top in this great nation while the rest of the world scrutinizes our misdeeds. Doth not our pride as a people urge us to improve our ways?

Create not an island of alien defense else its perimeter will be breeched by the outcasts of bigotry.

English ought to be the cord of unity in this nation o r else we grow pearls whose string can be broken.

Give a rap for your neighbor; your house may be on fire tomorrow.

The juggernaut of cruelty destroys the hapless animal. What gain is there?

If you must swagger do so before a mirror. because t he rest of the world will see your idiocy and laugh. Or, i n imitation thereof. overpopulate the world with heroes.

"Hav can I keep calm, sir. The seas are washing over the decks."

"Easy. Stay below."—from "The Beaufort Scale by Rat man Clymer, Bsn.

Never try to swing ship while she's tied up at the dock. You'll have a huge bill in damages to pay. This is much like a loveless marriage.

Throw all the vegies at the actor that you want to b e-cause he is a vegetarian. There are compensations, you know, and even acting has its fringe benefits.

Your security is within. Do not let time pressure you to forget your keys.

A government in crisis and faced with unpredictable calamities will adopt expedient measures,, Wartime is such acrisis. It is a temptation for the unprincipled in our Congress to extend those compromises in the name of liberty. That, (today, is the irony of the American Delusion, that a pragmatically expedient government, supported b an ill-advised liberal press, misinforms the public that the fire is not out, that the crisis still exists, that they mus t compromise their personal freedoms for the good of all when they are the alli.

Tainted evidence that would be unacceptable in a court o f law prevails in the News and Documentaries of the tiroes. One finds bias in the editing, negligence in the selection o f scenes, artifice in the use of camera techniques and plain, old deceit in the running commentary—which may or may not be the truth about what the viewers have witnessed. Quality photography redeems the adulterations .

A photographic scene can substitute for a class-conscious ceremony or a cultic ritual. It can have the power to purge and therefore substitute for Christ. It may be salvational, warping thoughts to fit the playwright's schema, or substi-tutional, leading to misbegotten fantasy, or, indeed, positional, subtly demanding that the viewers adopt an ideology-can stance.

Without canons of purpose a film story is merely a medium. But whose canons? one has a right to ask.

A good photograph has an outer significance and an inner spirit. The photographer's value system is apparent in the final print. Since photography is an emotional medium, the sharing is persuasive.

Anarchy is the rule of total self-indulgence. It is quite often the cudgel of adult brats. They are living the lie of total autonomy.

Much of modern art is Messianic—a borrowed concept its function and purpose being to change lives. I'm not sure this is completely so; parabolic art can accomplish the same end yet may be patently religious.

No work of art can live unless the indelible marks of the creator's imagination are evident in the finished form.

-10-

The State will always try to proselytize the arts. since they represent power and therefore constitute a threat to the State's existence. Art literature is the product of a divergent mind deluded by the fact of its intrinsic importance. Enforce conformity; yet the delusion r e~ mains because the fact is persuasive. Thereupon. prove that the fact is a pathological delusion—though the mind's will to believe is sound—and a sterility of creative thought comes to be regarded as the commendable virtue of sanity. Once endow the divergent qualities with a prescribed social function, the importance of the unique imagination is then by degrees made manifest by its scientific sanity, its circuitous dogma of resignation. Piecemeal can the State thus preempt the unique imagination of the artist/writer, by first destroying the human delusion and next, by bridling the sacred fact that governed his creative belief. The oligarchy of the Masses in this way transmutes a delusion into a State morality. This metamorphosis will come about readily enough so long as the American people continue to federalize the arts and promote the censorship by money power.

Dream images are symbols that connote other wide-aw a k e experiences, thoughts or feelings. They may not release. Instead, they may intensity the awakened thoughts.

Much that is vivid is tawdry, therefore concreteness <u>perse</u> is of no great value. Revelational purpose fortifies and gives substance to concrete images.

Much of poetry is narcissistic and contributes to self-worship. The feeling of power gotten thereby is seductive.

Immediate reference is a chief advantage of live drama. The fictionalist must conjure up the images perhaps t o an unwilling participant.

A trope, or figure of speech, can obscure a literary idea because it is inappropriate, or it can heighten the emotion of a character or mood of a scene because it augments; or then again the trope can deaden the effect o f a statement because it is nugatory, or intensify because it reflects similitudes of action or description.

The dimensions of a metaphorical image can be the obvious, the possible, the elusive and the fantastic

It is a poisonous literature that mocks certain universal virtues such as kindness, charity, honesty and forgiveness^ It does this by tricking out the virtue as a vice or an obsolete fashion.

Contemporary sitcomes invite you to invest your bad conscience in the wrong actions of the character portrayed .This is a pagan concept, the witchcraft of sin transfer. The god, or TV idol, takes on the mantle of your evil and is able to expunge it and thus cleanse you. Temple goddesses at one time performed this service. The reverse is that the god or goddess can invest one, the innocent, with an acceptr able code of conduct. The demigod functions as a spirit-trap, vanishing like an illusion (when the set is turned off) Small wonder it is that viewers become so attached to their idols, who leave their audiences with meaningless artifacts of the medium.

The practices of fraud against the intellect and deceit against the imagination are the special perversion of television. Thus it deals in sensational lies, whether a whisper or an explosion.

The Chinese communist revolution is a philosophy of Asiatic fatalism. It denies the potential of a harmonious mankind. Chinese communism and European socialism represent the dysfunctional appeal to circumstantial expedience and to force.

Comedy contains incongruity, embarrassment, repetition, surprise, frustration and coincidence. There is an element of the gamble in comedy that invites a bet on the outcome.

Insight without a corresponding benefit is not a quality of the soul. Virtue must furnish us with that insight which, in turn, becomes the benefit. The relationships f or m a ring of strength.

The worship of counterfeit political heroes is today t h e boon of demographers. As the illiterate population swell s from Third World countries, manufactured heroes obscure the real.

One wonders as the absolute authority of newscasters as perceived by their audiences. What they reveal each night is not of their own making or chosing yet they are demigods t millions of Americans.

In higher education there is a temptation to bolt from tradition. For this reason the public often associates riots and rebellion with learning.

Authority confers power but not always wisdom. Americans often worship the artifacts of power, little knowing from whence it came or its ligitimate uses. Thus in their fervor o f trust they are set-ups for scams.

Situation ethics is the contemporary anarchy against absolute values. Their denial leads to a meaningless living filled mainly with hedonistic pleasures. Suicide is frequently the end of the line.

It is a paradox if blind chance has produced life from non-life. Further, it is specious to assert without any conclusive proof that the infinitude of varieties of life were all somehow fashioned by needs, commands, instincts for survival when those laws which govern energy, mass and motion have never been consensually explained but are only supposed to have existed before time and after time. We there fore have a universe that is both rational and irrational, purposeful and yet chaotic. The secular scientist cannot have it both ways. Design—by what agency, by what power, why?

The prison system in the United States is today based on reform rather than retribution, on eliightenment instead o f punishment, on reason as opposed to revenge. It believes in the evolutionary goodness of men that is brought about b y significant changes in his environment.

Man's efforts to find God through his Reason have spawned a plethora of cults. They are dead constructs of his own imaginings. Empirically they seem to him reasonable. Sociologically, they are neutral. Spiritually, they are anachronisms from the beginnings of time when Man sought to rest o readiety link with God.

The god of mainline religions is the image of his reflect e d self in those ceremonies, ordinances and vows which he no longer believes in. The sacredness of the Eucharist is a dead issue with most. The resurrection is a legalistic myth invented to destroy Jewish hedgemony in Jerusalem. In his quandry, modern man finds that there can be no restoration, no repentence but only his own forgiveness of self.

America's worship of the God of Equality means that we must suppress the gifted and elevate the mediocre. A true democracy rests upon the continuation of the Mediocre; when any rise above that level democracy ceases and an elite develops. The equal validity of all values affirms the consistency o f the State and Church. To achieve total equality the State must level the superior, raise the inferior, eliminate the gifted, extol the ordinary and, im effect, deny the validity of evolution socially though accepting it biologically.

The cult of self-esteem reflects back what each person loves about himself or herself. Each person is his or her own hero. Why have we need for any others—except perhaps a sports god or a media goddess. Being divine, we can be reincarnated therefore <u>personality</u> is indestructable.

The leveling power of television is just becoming apparent to In another half century, a mongrel kind of English will; b e widely accepted. Conduct is already controlled by the "politically correct" standard. As for resolving a crisis or a moral dilemma, millions of Americans will have forgotten how, since they will, by then, have trashed God, ethical standards, absolute values of belief and conduct. Then. of course, the. will be able to flip on the set for their answers.

Higher Education is a construct upon the premise that reason is sufficient—an inheritance of the 18th Century Enlightenment. His, man's, sentimentality is his failure to notice the emptiness of his adoration.

America today is a picture culture. A pictographic culture will not comprehend traditional concepts of his history o r the writings of its great men. Already, the immediately understandable heroes for the growing numbers of illiteratesare those of action—sports figures—or of sensuality, the entertainment figures. They are comprehensible without thought. These new heroes will not be folk heroes emerging from a people's struggles but manufactured heroes born of a publicist's fantasy. Except for a few who will consider it priceless, American history will slip into limbo, and the counterfeit kingdom of the media divines will govera for a thousand years.

The vocabulary of the watching public grows smaller and smaller as schools turn out functional illiterates. In time, dramas may have to resort, fully, to street vernacular, patois, back-alley slang and physical sign language—signs indicate t h at that is our direction. Ideas are abstractions, and they will die in the decline of literacy, since the literate mind can grasp only objects of physical sense, *the* sensuous. This is retrogression into the ignorance and illiteracy of savages.

"I will become like a god in my resolve to unite enemies and plenty with starvation. disease with medicine, envy with gratification and goods." So think the Globalists of today.

It is not psychology that is the god but rather the ends to which that understanding is put, THE TRIUMPH OF THE HUMA N PSYCHE, the epistomological ME, the incontestable I AM. These credos usurp the throne of the God of old. Popular psychology thus becomes a trenching tool by which the disciple digs in for combat, the weapon of choice against the enemy o f faith and alienation.

There is a dilemma inherent in the communication between the television sitcom and the audience. The medium supposes that there is understanding, the audience suspects that there i s a fraud being perpetrated on them. Neither openly admits its position. The medium is derogatory of values, the pub lie is disdainful of their presentation.

To endure is not to be victorious. What then? Is brute survival the last Rubicon? What JLS the triumph of the human spirit?

Poisonous literature has the capacity to give pleasure, yet the criterion of pleasure as a consequence has no real value. Pleasure is transitory, elusive, subject to whim and fancy and custom. At worst, it is an offshoot of deeper aims o f the nihilists, the existentionalists, they who have acquiesced in the business of death. At best, pleasure from literature is an affirmation that life is good and worth living and embracing. A pathological delight in death is poi&onous unless satire mitigates or a rational irony iHumiliates. Much of contemporary literature is therefore suicidal in its perceptions and despairing in its narrow context.

Why ought a child to obey authority when there is no Love or caring behind it? Extreme forms of narcissism and low self-esteem develop out of this matrix. So much for the dysfunctional family and the poor performance of youth in our society.

Adults relive their childhoods in the extended tantrums o f petty-crime sprees. They merge any sense of wrongdoing with society's hedonistic drives.

Effective communication involves an agreement on the referents of speaker and listener, actor and audience, writer and reader. But, lacking this commonality, the presuppositions of one will not correspond to those of the other. Miscommunication results. The only way out of this impasse is when the creator's supposition of understanding becomes the recipient's acceptance of the truth of a proposition, a creative statement. The colossal fraud perpetrated by the television medium's drama beliongs to this dilemma resolution through propaganda. Sitcoms, for example, persuade a re luctant audience to gree with their views.

The photograph has no intrinsic value until historicity and notoriety endow it.

Photographs can either affirm or deny reason.

Primitive emotions of anger, revenge, lust and the like in-vest the media with the semblance of real life. Rarely is there any critical cognition or sensitivity refinement in a primieval silence.

Most practitioners of television drama are little removed Irom primitive cave drawings and the mores of phenomenological debasement. Their images convey basic instinct experiences by means of stereotypical conduct. This simplistic approach to American life makes possible formula writing and the ware-housing of character emotions,, of character face masks, a f character problems.

What is objectivity if it is not the total absence of any values? Yet the absence of the traditional values betrays a substitute system of moral anarchy. And its purveyors are those who would put their own values into place, assigni n g them to characters <u>they</u> deem good or bad. So long as the writers dominate the story it is propagandistic; so long as they oppress the characters to behave in a certain way, their writing is dishonest.

The salacious slander in the gossip of the "soaps" finds its true recognition and imitation in the minds of millions o f viewers. Much of video drama is therefore confessionaliin import.

The decision-makers of television are the wizards of defamation. Ratings only imply, they do not confirm a consensus.

The need of millions of Americans for vicarious risk affirms the validity of television violence.

Photography list

iconoclastic	utilitarian	revolutionizing
vicarious	entertaining	artificial
possessive	instructive	hypnotic
exorcistic	therapeutic	factual
remedial	propagandist	historical

Sleazy attempts at secular moralization fail to come off because the morals displayed via video are empty shed-skins of warehouses emotions. At the feet of these idols millions cone to pray each day, to pray that the baby is legitimate, that the lovely couple cohabit, that the doctor-father gets his comeuppance. Then the viewers pay their tcibute by the purchase of the product advertised. There is a primitive exorcision in these rites by the priests of power, the advertiser agents.

Acting schools perpetuate stereotypes of performance, presenting what audiences expect. Character depictions often have little to do with character but are contrivances only. Artificial grimaces, responses, inflections, motives thus attain the stature of the liturgical in <u>sitcoms</u> and <u>soaps</u>. The spell cast is renewed each day.

Television contains a leveling power that is not yetfully apparent, that leads to conformity elementally—psychologically, emotionally, intellectually, physically, and spiritually. English is mongrelized. Personal conduct is trivialized. Thought is controlled—all that we might get along with the rest of the world whom we have so selfishly ignored.

-11-

In poetry meter is patterned rhythm, but rhythm is more than accent/ unaccent. Rhythm is (1) sound repetition, (2) regularity of variables, e.g. 1st and 3rd lines of a 4-stan z a poem can have a varied foot; (3)rhythm is ebb and flow of at poem's strongest emotion or emotionally evocative words, (4) is the patterned juxtaposition of abstract and concrete wands. Rhythm is (5) the pleasing use of spaced rests, (6) the association of similar vowel sounds internal to the poem, and (7) the alternation of consonance and assonance.

The messianic nature of today's education bears its own seeds of destruction because children are being taught that before adulthood, living experientially comes s elf-esteem, before accomplishment comes self-indulgence and before understandling comes feeling. Old concepts of sacrifice, of commitment, of dedication, of life investment in purpose are being demolished and with them the value-system of our Judeo-Christian heritage.

Religion inevitably has for its contemporary idol the MAN-IMAGE, the prophet surrounded by doctrines of deception . The Pope and his church, the secularist evangel, the renegade who forms a distant colony, the practioners of those cults that establish themselves as minor sects and demand worship of their gods.

NINE SIGNS AND EVIDENCES:
1) Money buys in, self-indulgence promoted
2) Wealth, power, satisfaction in this world are rigjitr-fully yours
3) Works as a means to sanctification
4) Escapism rampant
5) Consecration comes with purchase of bibles, certificates and memberships

6) transliteration of small money into great events, omens and the transcendant lifestyle.
7) Reverential meditation with the mind focused upon Self.
8) Promises without fulfillment
9) Creeds self-fulfillment without effort
   Litany surrender to my appeals
   bow your knee to my superior force
   prophets are followers who have arrived
   evidence is paid testimonials
   Doctrine man can achieve self-fullment by concentrating on himself, letting Force work through him (New Age)
   - faith is essential
   - practice is essential
   - all negative thoughts are superstition bewitchery, evil and unproductive.
   - native American independence is extrapolated into independence from God
   - outward individualism has become self emulation internalized, leading to total autonomy—or, anarchy.

Television is a medium of vicarious risk-taking.

As pecuniary gain comes to dominate personal integrity in in this country, more and more people begin to share the mindset of the thief, the extortionist, the slanderer t o whom integrity means nothing.

The god of higher education is not a desire to learn but a drive to dominate, euphemistically called "winning." Ye t that dominion issues from power founded on status. The dominion is rarely with the sword of truth but more often with the club of possessions.

Higher education is the epistem. Logical failure of reason as the final solution to human happiness.

Men scramble wildly about in their dazed condition, searching for reassurances as to their personal worth, their location among the masses of humanity. They are to be pitied.

The will not to succeed but to fail is with us, for the acceptance of failure is, in effect, a self-forgiveness for the absence of effort, ambition, goals, values. Blaming not their own lack of effort and motivation, youth and adults sink into the ennui-laden oblivion of defeat. They are fitting targets for a welfare government.

Self-gratification is father to violence. It is hedonistic.

Most men would prefer to gratify their own goodness rather than God's. What can be more intimate than Self?

The success of cults appears to justify the investment o f trust in their ritual and doctrines. But do they change men's ways or only their perception of circumstances?

The removal of pain and the satisfactions of the body r u le the persuasions of commerce.

It is blasphemous to sympathize with widows and speak for the unborn without raising a hand. or voicing a protest t o help.

The will to believe is the acceptance of the gamble on t h e unknown. Technological knowing is the reduction of the gamble-risk. Believe in the results of diminished risk and the will to believe turns to what can be manipulated. Therefore, God is unnecessary. Condition people as masses t o accept the diminished risk and they become conditioned t o accept the will to believe as rational only when based o n the functional. Give them the technological leadership to manipulate the functional and they transfer the will to believe in an unknowable God to a knowable environment and its technicians. Technology then becomes god to lift u p the massese. Religion and the intelligensia, the elite, ply this metamorphosis of thought in our schools.

Escapism is responsibility avoidance whose ends are the neglect of acceptable social conduct—non-criminal a n d non-injurious—and societal disapproval. Escapism b a t-tens on the opprobrium that its devotees attach to what is constant in life. Escapism searches out hidden caverns for practice, bowers of self-indulgence. the images of excitement and novelty. the wish-thinking of imaginary retreats. Escapism is not just a fetish but a crystalic vision of illusory changes that ought to last but cannot. The ambivalence of escapism is schizoid; it is suicidal and catatonic, productive of death and nothingness. Escapism i s an endless trail into a borderless desert.

The rebuke of a parent's authority by his child is often a realistic substitute of the latter's inherent goodness. Yet often, too, rejection of parental teachings leaves a vacuum which peer pressure, pain and cultic savagery hasten to fill, at the same time dealing out tranquilizlng drugs and an unintelligible racket called "music." How then can attempts at enlightenment dispel the psychedelic shadows?

The screaming, wild-animal aspect of acid rock music is not only prurient and violent. Its sedative effets quiet criticism; its erotic nature is that of animals in seasonal heat or on a stampede. For its practitioners, it is power. For its followers it is submission to impulse, instinct. For its devotees it is cultic.

The politicization of sexual deviation, tricked out a s "lifestyles," converts the legislatures of state and n action into arenas where old values are thrown to the bestial. Apart from the spectacle of debasing what was once traditional, the Senators accept a standard that demean s their stature as men, yet since they are accountable mainly to themselves, they will not be coerced into making comparisons. To cast a vote for the perverse is to diefy what is detestable to a majority and to open the way for a plurality of corruptions of mind, bosy and spirit.

Convenience as an abstract concept in America is idolatrous and spell-binding. The buzz-word is an icon that will brook no attacks. Convenience is central to the lives o f many.

A cavalier willingness to hold up the redemptive nature o f our judicial system drives many worthy judges to rely o n therapeutic "retribution" that would save the criminal a t the expense of the victims and their pain and loss.

A tacit belief in order lies behind all retribution a n d therefore in the efficacy of the law. The efficacy of our laws weakens to the extent that retributive punishment i s c omproraised.

Higher education is an irrational extension of the need for an educated society in a democratic Republic. Unattainable by most it tends, when unduly stressed. to quench the desire for rudimentary learning.

A college degree confers a priesthood status upon the naive. Having ignored the humanities as disciplines they usually ignore the nature of the beast. knowing much about popular psychology and its manipulative techniques but little about, inner spiritual needs. For after all, what is <u>spirit</u>? I s it "go team," or a feeling of inner emptiness?

There's a seed of destruction in laziness: the denial o f capacity and potential and seeing all as worthless gain Religiosity can have this pernicious effect when emphasizing the "after life," the other world. Such an attitude mocks the God who meted out talents.

America's lapse into barbarism is rather like a retreat into the Middle Ages—with her carnalities of the clergy, the torture of limitless litigation, the phoney passes at justice by headsmen of the courts, the defecation upon a value system that brought enlightened legislation and a civil government beneficial to the whole world. Integrity and honesty in high places have become mere tricks of the imag inaction, cavalier chimeras of "decency."

Macho, as a concept, perpetuates the notion of <u>death</u> t o manliness through its practices of reprisal, force and violence. It tolerates no subjective abasement, no humility, no discussion of alternatives and no comprehension of what is truly feminine. <u>Macho</u> is absolute, extremist and steeped in the lore of false honor and justifiable homicide. I t is satanic and malevolent and considers discovery, obedience and chastity as obsolete and worthless and unbecoming to the male image. <u>Macho</u> stands for recognition only of the narcissistic image, that and that alone to qualify for its cloak.

Where once youngsters were nurtured into manhood and womanhood, today their flowering is corrupted into lifestyle s that debase virtue as frivolous and obsolete, morality a s chimerical and oppressive commitment to a cause, to another person, to the family. Such commitments are inconsequential and values of honest, integrity and honor are seen as the cherished woodrot of Judeo-Christian slavery. Those who crusade to destroy the value structure of an earlier America would replace its force and power in lives with the simplistic pleasure-pain standard.

POWER, whether political, physical or spiritual, takes its form in the manipulation of people, in kinds of violence for entertainment and in religious showmanship and the cult of reincarnation borrowed from Hindooism. To be deprives o f POWER—is impotence. POWER, when seized or acquired, a f-firms one's worth as a human being. It is ahared only out of necessity. POWER protects, it rewards for labor an d effort. POWER brings into reality dreams and visions. POW-er sets us apart, a chosen few, fated to lead or at leatst to rise above the ruck of humanity. POWER condemns those who are against its holders, the united dissimilar person alities. PGVER disenfranchizes those who disrupt its sway and direction. POWER enobles, glorifies, elevates, gratifies, rewards and protects. For these reasons POWER for many is desireable and its means to acquiring it sacrificial.

Experience, not escape, tricks and traps the firsttime user of drugs. Its use is a fetish that sets one apart, substituting, as it does, the experience for sober exploratio, n into the unknown. That S-a d experience is illusory because it replaces real experience, substituting the euphoria o f submission for the reality of risk, and accepting the possibility of death not as the result of struggle but of surrender. Through his visions the drug user has lost control o f reality. He has receeded into the twilight of existentialnon-feeling. He has achieved death without cutting t he cord of life. He has exhibited a pitilessness in his sacrifice of "me."

Drugs separate man from God by the insertion of a chasm, a vacuum of non-cognition which takes place when the euphoria reaches its climax. In that state of mindm man has cease d to be man even to the extent of communicating with himself. Furthermore, feelings of pain which he hastned to obliterate do not register as thought. He is as close to being s mere vegetable as he can ever get, short of destroying portions of his motor-sensory brain. He merely exists, he has mass, shape, a voice as such to indicate that he is a mortal, but little else besides. Disconnected would be the right descriptive word. At this juncture he is vulnerable to demonis influence and parascientific invasions.

The future of America is undermined and jeopardized by drugs within the drugged generation. They have withdrawn from life, just as their parents have withdrawn from life on alcohol.

Death is a litany of satan. Its creed is the defiance of death without Christ. It finds fitting surrogacy in watching others die. Any "salvation" must come by chance, fate, curcumstances, all shibboleths of chaos. Satans promotion of death attributes his own values to human life. He at tempts to deceive and then to manipulate the will—as in euthanasia. He would have men embrace death as escape. To satan death sanctifies, promotes "wisdom," knowledge, etc thus "one man's return from death; is a popular topic. H e promotes the notion that death heals, thus we have the erring soul who is healed through karma. Death, to t h e evil angel, invites trial, insinuates immortality, m imics surrender to him. To hell's ruler, death is forgiving o f life, is salvational, judgemental, abhoring efforts to impede or deter or deny its credibility. Death, to the prince of dearkness, is retributive, vindicating itself by t h e narcissism latent in the suicidal person. Demons are presented as kind to man, totally rational beings, the catalytic agents who hide the spiritual schism between t h e saved and the damned.

In sports where winning is everything, mercenaries play the game. It is surrogate combat, legalized violence and a form of substitutionary salvation. Professional sports expunge uncontrollable fate, exorcise hatred for losers and promote a sentimental condescension toward losers. In professional sports, enmity is acceptable and obeisance t o chance, god of winning and money and success. Professional! sports belongs in the pantheon of the gods, the rules o f the game dispelling <u>chance</u>. The combat restores feelings of innocence to the victor, imparts "guilt" to the loser.

In professional sports. "love for the game" becomes meaning-less.

Chaos may be dramatic but it is not drama. The formlessness is a vanity that keeps a playwright from imposing his own mind on the raw materials of life. Yet that attitude is one of false humility. He lives and observes by t h e philosophy of <u>incidentalism</u>. shot through with the meaning-lessness of the incidents.

Living things have form. Why not art?

The catastrophe of much of modern-day photography is that it presents effects as relevant to life and living. One may as well! stare with studied scrutiny at the fractured images and kaleidoscopic lights of the merry-go-round.

Write a good book, entertain your soul.

Do not keep a friend waiting for your compliment. It will seem insincere if stale.

Friendship does not barter away the intimacies of nearness, but instead respects them.

Wisdom is only a tool. It should be used with care.